I've Seen It All at the Library

I've Seen It All at the Library

The View from Behind the Desk

Jonathan M. Farlow

McFarland & Company, Inc., Publishers
Jefferson, North Carolina

LIBRARY OF CONGRESS CATALOGUING-IN-PUBLICATION DATA

Farlow, Jonathan, 1969–
I've seen it all at the library : the view from behind the desk / Jonathan M. Farlow.
    p. cm.
Includes bibliographical references and index.

ISBN 978-0-7864-9684-6 (softcover : acid free paper) ∞
ISBN 978-1-4766-1874-6 (ebook)

1. Farlow, Jonathan, 1969–   2. Public librarians—North Carolina—Biography.
3. Public libraries—North Carolina—Anecdotes.   I. Title.

Z720.F28A3 2015   020.92—dc23   [B]   2015005454

BRITISH LIBRARY CATALOGUING DATA ARE AVAILABLE

© 2015 Jonathan M. Farlow. All rights reserved

No part of this book may be reproduced or transmitted in any form or by any means, electronic or mechanical, including photocopying or recording, or by any information storage and retrieval system, without permission in writing from the publisher.

Cover image © iStock/Thinkstock

Printed in the United States of America

*McFarland & Company, Inc., Publishers
Box 611, Jefferson, North Carolina 28640
www.mcfarlandpub.com*

To librarians everywhere,
past, present and future.

Table of Contents

Acknowledgments 9
Introduction 11

1. Laser Tag in the Library 21
2. Library 101 32
   ❖ *Unknown Library Firsts* 52
3. Let's Move the Library 53
   ❖ *Things to Remember When Moving Your Library* 66
4. Library School, Finally! 67
   ❖ *Classes They Should Teach in Library School* 74
   ❖ *Jon's Nine Circles of Library Hell* 75
5. I Am the Law! 76
6. The Future Is Now 81
   ❖ *How to Tell If a Patron Is Viewing Porn as Opposed to a Nude* 92
7. Does Your Family Tree Fork? 93
   ❖ *Things Never to Say to a Librarian* 105
8. The Brotherhood/Sisterhood of the Book 106
9. Oh, Christmas Tree 118
10. Rats 122

Table of Contents

11. The Brief Reign of Pharaoh Ho-Ho and the Queen of Denial 136
12. Working at the Mayberry Library 144
13. Potty Humor in the Library 149
    ❖ *Things Librarians Would Love to Say to Their Patrons* 155
14. Goodbye 156

Appendix A: Library Stories 161
Appendix B: A Letter to Library Patrons or Prospective Patrons 175
Appendix C: A Letter to My Fellow Librarians 177
Bibliography 181
Index 183

Acknowledgments

Priscilla Oldaker, the A, number one, world's best editor in the whole wide world. (No, the preceding sentence was not grammatically correct.)

Lori Tart	Sarah Hudson	Robin Buchanan
Jessica Schaefer	Kim Steelman	Shirley McKinney
Eric Compean	Christina Adams	Sheila Killebrew
Ruth Ann Copley	Robin Shuman	Ross Holt
Matt Shaw	Marsha Haithcock	Dave Bare
Warren Dixon	Ken Coleman	

And last but not least, Queenie. Is Heaven clean enough yet?

I sincerely hope that I haven't forgotten anyone. If you feel that you belong on this list, you do.

"There are naïve questions, tedious questions, ill-phrased questions, questions put after inadequate self-criticism. But every question is a cry to understand the world. There is no such thing as a dumb question."
—Carl Sagan

"I don't believe in colleges and universities. I believe in libraries because most students don't have any money. When I graduated from high school, it was during the Depression and we had no money. I couldn't go to college, so I went to the library three days a week for 10 years."
—Ray Bradbury

"Librarians are the coolest people out there doing the hardest job out there on the frontlines. And every time I get to encounter or work with librarians, I'm always impressed by their sheer awesomeness."
—Neil Gaiman

"Libraries should be open to all—except the censor."—John F. Kennedy

"You see, I don't believe that libraries should be drab places where people sit in silence, and that's been the main reason for our policy of employing wild animals as librarians."—Graham Chapman

"For him that stealeth a book from this library, let it change into a serpent in his hand and rend him. Let him be struck with palsy, and all his members blasted. Let him languish in pain crying aloud for mercy, and let there be no surcease to his agony till he sink to dissolution. Let bookworms gnaw his entrails in token of the worm that dieth not, and when at last he goeth to his final punishment, let the flames of Hell consume him for ever and aye."
—Anonymous, The Monastery of San Pedro, Barcelona

Introduction

There's a funny scene in the movie *Monsters University* where the main characters are competing in some sort of wacky Olympics or zany decathlon. During one event they are supposed to sneak through a library without making any noise, thus avoiding the ire of the tentacled librarian who sits behind the front desk, glowering. I thought that scene was the funniest of the movie not because there were monsters in the library instead of people, or because the librarian was a monstrous combination of a snail and an octopus whose eyes were on the ends of stalks and her glasses on the end of a long wand. No, it's the fact that they're in a library and it's actually quiet. Maybe it's different in academic libraries, but if memory serves me right, it's not. There are times in public libraries that I wouldn't have noticed a bunch of monsters sneaking through the reading room. In fact, there are days when I would welcome it.

It is funny that people's views of a lot of things have changed dramatically over the years but their visions of libraries haven't changed that much. Every library that appears in commercials, TV shows or movies is a staid, quiet place with people reading studiously, under the glare of a sour-looking old bat with half-moon glasses and her hair in a bun. Comedian Paula Poundstone stated, "It's funny that we think of libraries as quiet demure places where we are shushed by dusty bun-balancing bespectacled women. The truth is libraries are raucous clubhouses for free speech, controversy and community. Librarians have stood up to the Patriot Act, sat down with noisy toddlers and reached out to illiterate adults. Libraries can never be shushed." Peter Griffin from *Family Guy* said that libraries are places where homeless men go to move their bowels. To be quite honest, both statements are true, but I would like to think that the former is closer to the truth.

First, the bowel thing. Yes, a great many public librarians have walked into the public restrooms and been hit by a semi-solid wall of stench and the sight of a pair of ratty-looking feet under a stall door—that is, if their eyes are not burned out of their sockets by a naked man, or woman, bathing in the sink. Still, as Ms. Poundstone puts it, libraries are not "quiet and demure"; if you want quiet and demure, maybe a junior league cotillion or a funeral home will be to your liking, but not a library, not anymore. The "raucous clubhouse" fits better and librarians are among the biggest advocates of freedom of expression that I know of. They serve their community not just by providing books but by providing education, by providing a gateway to a new job, skill, degree or, sometimes, a complete change of lifestyle. Has there been controversy? Oh, yes, but there have also been countless story times, library programs and book sales. Libraries have definitely changed as they have moved into the modern era. Still, however, the stereotype has not changed. It's so ingrained in our culture that if a future civilization were to come upon the remnants of ours, long since destroyed, in and among all the wreckage of our dead world, it would be some sort of image of a bespectacled woman, with her hair in a bun, glasses sliding down her nose and her finger to her mouth shushing some ancient and unseen library patron.

Let's delve into this stereotype a little more, just in case the reader has been meditating on a mountain in Tibet or sleeping under a rock somewhere. Most of the time this creature is female, of sour disposition and draconian in enforcing the myriad rules and regulations that she has put in place for the sole purpose of making the lives of her patrons all the more difficult. Truly, beneath the cardigan sweater, the old-lady flower print dress, and the bra that hasn't been unclasped by anyone else but her since the Reagan administration, beats the heart of a tyrant. Appearance-wise she's thin, not athletic, trim, but bony, crone-like. Think the Wicked Witch of the West with glasses. Then there's the trademark bun which, unbeknownst to most people, pulls the librarian's hair back with the same tension as those cables that hold up circus tents. And what of the male librarians, effete milquetoasts, just as thin as the women with necks like giraffes, in corduroys, sweaters and *Star Trek* belt buckles, mincing around the reference area like storks in penny loafers.

In my research a great majority of the librarians in popular culture fall into four distinct categories. The description that I have just provided is the first and most familiar. Dealings with these librarians are hardly ever pleasant. These creatures are picky and bad tempered. Think of Madam Pince from the Harry Potter books who's described as "a thin, irritable woman who looked like an underfed vulture" or the librarian in the movie *Sophie's Choice*, played by John Rothman, who barks at Sophie Zawistowski (Meryl Streep), "Do you want me to draw you a map?" Hollywood doesn't seem to have a very pleasurable view of the library as a place to work. In *It's a Wonderful Life*, as Jimmy Stewart is shown how hellish life would be without him, what is the horrible fate awaiting his wife? *Dear God, she's closing the library!*

At least in film this stereotype is an old one. I've already mentioned *It's a Wonderful Life* which was released in 1946. The earliest movie that I was able to find mention of a librarian as a minor character is *The Philadelphia Story*, 1940. A tabloid reporter is attempting to dig up some dirt on a wealthy socialite as well as her prominent family. In this, the pre–Internet days of the late 30s or early 40s, the material will be obtained at the public library. There we are introduced to the librarian, a middle-aged woman with a bun and high collar who speaks like an eighteenth-century Quaker.

"What is thy wish?" She groans in one scene, and "If thee will consult with my colleague in there" in another. Lo and behold the reporter finds none other than said socialite, demurely reading a book. He strikes up a conversation and the two start making small talk, drawing the most famous library word of them all from the librarian: "Shhhhhh!"

The following year saw the release of *Citizen Kane*, a movie that a lot of supposed experts regard as one of the greatest movies ever made. Still there is a scene in a library. Reporters go to this library looking for the journal of Walter Parks Thatcher, Charles Foster Kane's childhood guardian, to see if the word "Rosebud" held any importance in the late industrialist's life. The librarian's name is Miss Anderson. Sure enough, she is clad in Bible black with glasses and slicked back hair the color of coal. She is impatient and pretentious in the extreme, often ignoring what the reporter—that is, the patron—is saying to her.

In 1946's *The Big Sleep* Humphrey Bogart has a run-in with a blonde-haired old harpy in a white collar at the Hollywood Public Library. Bogart's character is looking for information on first edition books, drawing a comment from the service-minded librarian that he doesn't look like the kind of man who is interested in first editions. Bogart comes back with "Yeah, I collect blondes in bottles too." Obviously this is meant to be an insult although it is fairly tame when you compare it to the kind of zingers that are thrown back and forth in movies these days. The next year saw the release of the musical *Good News*, the story of a football star whose love interest, Connie, works in the library. Like *It's a Wonderful Life*, the movie does not paint a very favorable view of those people who are dragged kicking and screaming into the library and chained to the reference desk. When the main character asks the object of his affection why she works in the library, her reply is, "Oh, it helps pay my tuition. It's something called working your way through college." Connie is actually very pleasant, very upbeat and very pretty. A good representation of librarians, you're thinking; however, remember,

Connie is just a student worker. Her supervisor—the actual librarian—is the same old gargoyle that we have seen in other films. She's sixtyish with a grayish bun, hissing, "Shhhh." When Connie is ready for the prom she asks a friend how she looks and the friend responds that she doesn't look like a librarian. Does Connie rise to defend her bookish comrades? No. How does she respond? By saying: "Oh, I don't feel like one."

I'll go ahead and include Marian the Librarian from *The Music Man*. Shirley Jones played her in the 1962 film version, but, despite her mousy demeanor, I don't know if I would call her the stereotypical librarian because very few of them sing and dance in the library and fall in love with con men.

In the following paragraphs I'll give you some different looks at librarians, but I still have to wonder why the image that I have just detailed is so solidly entrenched in our mindset and our culture and has changed so little. *The Philadelphia Story* came out in 1940, *Monsters University* was released in 2013—that's 73 years and the mental image has stayed largely the same. Think about how our vision of mailmen has changed throughout the years. Once upon a time they were viewed as the smiling, friendly men who delivered our mail, in clean, pressed uniforms sort of like Mr. McFeely on *Mister Rogers' Neighborhood*. Now they're more like Newman from *Seinfeld*—out of shape, stupid and pissed off—who would sooner hide mail in a storage unit than deliver it to the people who are supposed to get it. The image of priests and clergy has also changed dramatically. Think about Spencer Tracy's character in the 1938 movie *Boys Town*. He's a kind, earnest soul who is honestly trying to better the lives of the boys who are in his charge with no illicit or alternative motives in mind. These days, when a pastor or padre is in a movie or TV show, he's at the least corrupt, lining his pockets with money from the collection plate, and at the most he's in league with the devil, killing and raping indiscriminately. Have there been bad priests in movies before this past decade? Sure, but *Jamaica Inn* (1939) changed the evil priest depicted in the book to an evil squire to avoid the violation of a production code that forbade painting the clergy in a negative light. In *The Night of the Hunter* (1955), Robert Mitchum played a Deep South preacher with a singing voice as smooth as silk and tattooed knuckles who slits Shelley Winters' throat. Recently, however, it seems like if there is a holy man in a movie or on television, except for the Hallmark Channel or some such avenue, he's some corrupt sicko. In *Doubt* (2008) Philip Seymour Hoffman's character may or may not have had indecent relations with a teenage boy. In *The Last Exorcism* (2010), a local pastor worships the devil and impregnates a teenage girl with some sort of monster. You can see the difference between *Boys Town* and *The Last Exorcism* in their portrayal of the clergy, but the difference between *The Philadelphia Story* and *Monsters University* is very narrow. Do I have any answers to the quandary regarding librarians in these movies? No, I don't. I can, however, offer a couple of exceptions.

The second type of pop culture librarian is the librarian as scenery. She's a living backdrop to the actual action where you can see her going about her duties as the heroes hold our attention, most of the time as she's stamping something. In *The Big Sleep*, while Humphrey Bogart is butting heads with the blonde librarian, there is a co-worker in the background who serves as nothing more than a complement to the back wall. In *Indiana Jones and the Last Crusade*, the main character and his cohorts are trying to enter the catacombs beneath Venice through the library. As Indiana Jones drags over a short brass pole, the kind that holds up velvet ropes, and proceeds to bash it into the marble floor, we cut to the mousy male librarian with a bow tie and an Albert Einstein hairdo. Just as he hits the paper with his stamp, Jones hits the floor with the pole, which makes it sound like his rubber stamp is ringing out with the clamor of metal on stone. The poor guy studies the stamp like a monkey doing a math problem, we all have a good laugh at his expense, and he is pushed into the background and out of our memories as Jones goes on to hunt for the holy grail.

The last two types are a lot rarer, but prevalent and important nevertheless. The third kind in our list is the sexy librarian. I once had a friend ask me if I knew any sexy librarians. I very sarcastically answered him like he had asked if I had ever seen Bigfoot. "Well, I've been told they exist," I said. "But I think they're a myth. I've seen some bad photos and some grainy film but no ironclad evidence." In direct contrast to the stereotypical bookish, introverted librarian, I have heard from a couple of semi-reliable sources that one of the top role-playing fantasies for men involves a librarian complete with the glasses and the bun. There's a funny sequence in the movie *Porky's II* where some of the over-sexed teenagers from the first movie try to get back at some of the other over-sexed teenagers who pulled a prank on them in the previous film. The prank involved getting the prospective victims into a graveyard where they will be scared out of their wits by someone dressed as a ghoul who pops out of a false grave. They are lured out into said cemetery by the promise of a tryst with a nubile young lady named Graveyard Gloria who apparently gets uncontrollably horny whenever she enters a graveyard. The guys pick Gloria up where she works—you guessed it—the library. When they get her to the graveyard, sure enough, she starts ripping off her clothes and appears to be up for anything. Things don't go as planned, however, the tables get turned on the pranksters and one ends up running in the nude down the same road he did in the first movie. This fantasy plays on the hopeful fantasies of certain men, that in the heart of every meek, mild-mannered librarian is a raging nympho just waiting for the right man to lure her out. What about the male librarians? Can the fantasies of the ladies be satisfied among the ranks of male librarians? Well, I can answer that with a little sexy librarian history. Giacomo Girolamo Casanova was an Italian adventurer and author, born in 1725. He has also been regarded as one of the greatest lovers and most notorious womanizers in history. His name is synonymous with hot-blooded romance. When Casanova died in 1798, he was the librarian to Count Joseph Karl von Waldstein, a chamberlain of the emperor of Bohemia, now present-day Czech Republic.

The fourth and last type of pop culture librarian is the rarest but also the best, the kick-ass librarian. That librarian who defies stereotype and, in and among shelving books and answering reference questions, does something to justify his or her entrance into the annals of bad assery. Sadly, I was not able to find any historical figures who fit the modern model of a kick-ass librarian. True, there are a great many people who were at one time or another librarians and who have done a great deal to defy the stereotype of the quiet librarian in the corner. Benjamin Franklin, Mao Tse-Tung, J. Edgar Hoover and Casanova come to mind, but I don't think I would call them kick-ass librarians, so I have stuck with their fictional counterparts. Also, I am sure that there are librarians who are not famous who have done things that put them in this category, but I am sticking with names the average person will be able to recall.

The first kick-ass librarian that I can remember is Barbara Gordon. She is the daughter of Commissioner Gordon who serves as a liaison of sorts between Batman and the Gotham City Police Department. Barbara was played by Yvonne Craig in the campy '60s *Batman* TV series, and some time during the show's run she decided to supplement her time as a public librarian by donning cap and cowl and becoming Batgirl. The character itself was created by DC Comics in 1961, along with a character named Batwoman as a move to counteract accusations of a homoerotic subtext in the *Batman* series by Fredric Wertham in his book *Seduction of the Innocent*, because everybody knows that two gay men can't exist alongside a couple of hot chicks. In a touch of irony, the character of Batwoman is now one of the few comic characters who is an outed lesbian. At first, Batgirl's secret identity was a woman named Betty Kane, but in 1967 the character was rewritten and her nom de guerre was switched to Barbara Gordon, a librarian. Over the years Barbara Gordon obtained her doctorate in library science, became the director of the Gotham library and was elected to Congress. On the superhero front she was shot by the Joker and rendered a paraplegic. Afterwards she became the "information broker" known as the Oracle who heads the female superhero team, the Birds of Prey.

The heroine of the 1999 remake of *The Mummy* is Evelyn "Evy" Carnahan, played by Rachel Weisz, a Cairo librarian who starts the movie dubiously by destroying the library where she works by knocking all the shelves over, domino style. The director says something to her that nobody wants to hear: "Tell me again why I let you work here?" After meeting her future husband, Rick O'Connell (Brendan Fraser), and heading into the desert after the lost city of Hamunaptra, Evy deals with all the plagues of Egypt—flesh eating scarabs, Americans, booby traps and an amorous mummy who kidnaps her in an attempt to bring his lady love back from the dead. On the way Evy gets drunk and makes the best declaration of her profession in the history of mankind.

> EVY: You're wondering, "What is a place like me doing in a girl like this?"
> RICK: Yeah, something like that.
> EVY: Look, I ... I may not be an explorer, or an adventurer, or a treasure-seeker, or a gunfighter, Mr. O'Connell, but I am proud of what I am.
> RICK: And what is that?
> EVY: I ... am a librarian.

Then she passes out.

There is also a series of TV movies entitled *The Librarian* where the main character, played by Noah Wyle, is charged with caring for such legendary items as Pandora's Box, Tesla's Death Ray, the Holy Grail, the transmuted corpse of King Midas, the Ark of the Covenant, the Golden Fleece, a live unicorn, the Goose That Laid the Golden Eggs, Excalibur, the original Mona Lisa (as it turns out the one in the Louvre is a copy), the original "Little Boy" prototype atomic bomb, a working jet pack, Ali Baba's Flying Carpet, and a piece of the Spear of Destiny, which forms the basis of the first movie. In this first chapter, Flynn Carsen is a professional student with 22 academic degrees. He is kicked out of college by a professor who tells him to get some real life experience. He receives an invitation for an interview at the Metropolitan Public Library where a couple of the attending librarians, Jane Curtin and Bob Newhart, show him this iconic collection. He is told that he will not only care for the magic items in his charge but protect them. Soon the Spear of Destiny is stolen by the Serpent Brotherhood. Whoever has the entire spear, three pieces, can control the destiny of the world. Using only a mysterious book and his wits, the librarian must track down the remaining two pieces of the spear before the brotherhood does.

In the sequel, which occurs a year after the first Carsen's collection has expanded to include the head of Medusa, the trident of Poseidon, the Shroud of Turin and the Pipes of Pan, he is ambushed at his apartment and robbed of a scroll that he received in the mail. As it turns out, the scroll contains the directions to King Solomon's mines and the Book of Solomon, which is hidden in the mines, and will give the bearer control over time and space. In typical swashbuckling fashion, Carsen saves the day in a scenario that involves, indirectly, his long lost father as well as his uncle. The book is thrown into molten lava. The next chapter involves the Philosopher's Stone as well as the Judas Chalice, an artifact which is formed from the 30 pieces of silver that Judas was paid for betraying Christ. An ex–KGB agent wants to use the chalice to resurrect Prince Vlad Dracula. There is the typical amount of action and daring and you can probably guess what happens in the end. I have seen bits and pieces of *The Librarian* movies, but I am not a huge fan. I am somewhat insulted, however, because whenever my wife hears of an action movie franchise featuring a swashbuckling librarian, she bursts out laughing.

On the TV series *Buffy the Vampire Slayer*, Buffy's mentor is a school librarian named Rupert Giles. Giles is a Watcher. A Watcher is part of an ancient and secret organization charged with preparing the Slayer to battle demonic forces. A Slayer is a girl born into each generation who is bestowed with the essence of a demon and given various powers, such as super strength, agility, resistance to damage and the ability to look wonderful even in the toughest situations. As a Watcher, Giles has an extensive knowledge of magic, decent combat skills—including a knowledge of Jujitsu and Aikido—proficiency in several languages and a willingness to do almost anything, even kill, to achieve his mission. He also has a background as a rock and roll musician and apparently he's also somewhat of a lothario, even romancing Buffy's mother at some point.

I've been told by more than one librarian that one of the ultimate library movies is *Desk Set*, a 1957 film with Katharine Hepburn and Spencer Tracy. Hepburn is Bunny Watson, a reference librarian at Federal Broadcasting Network. The company is negotiating a merger, but is keeping it on the down low. The higher-ups have foreseen a dramatic rise in the amount of work for their librarians and have decided to bring in two computers that will supposedly help ease the workload of the library staff. Richard Sumner, Tracy, is the computer expert who observes at the library to figure out how there can be an easy transition to bringing in the "electronic brains," as they are called in the movie. The library staff is afraid that the computers are there to replace them, which isn't true, but their assumptions are seemingly supported when the electronic brains mistakenly send pink slips to everyone in the company, including the president. A romantic game of cat and mouse erupts between Watson and Sumner, which is complicated by the fact that Watson believes Sumner will always rate his computers higher than her. She puts this theory to the test when she rigs one of the computers to self-destruct, a pretty badass move, betting that Sumner won't be able to resist fixing it. He does give in and repairs the computer, but Watson gives in as well and they end the movie on a romantic note.

Introduction

Does the fact that these exceptions exist mean that somebody somewhere believes that librarians can be more than book jockeys, or are they making these characters librarians because of some sense of irony, to make a subtle joke at our expense? Regardless, the average everyday person thinks of libraries as cold, quiet institutions where books are kept and nothing more. Who knows, if I wasn't a librarian I might have thought the same thing. I have met librarians who have fallen into the previously mentioned categories. No, I will not tell you who the sexy librarians are. I have come to know these people quite well and, for the most part, mousy or demure is not how I would classify them. Yes, some fit into these categories, yet others defy description. I hope you will come to know this by reading this book.

As it is, the library has become a home away from home. When I first started my career, Bill Clinton was our new president, the Branch Davidians had just been burned out of their complex in Texas, and Monica Seles was stabbed in the back by a crazed fan during a tennis match. The big reference question when I started concerned a short story by Dell James called "November Rain," which supposedly inspired the video for the Guns and Roses song of the same name. I had just barely graduated college and was engaged to be married. In the next twenty years I grew a lot as a person, as a writer and as a librarian. Libraries changed as well. Their technology went from CD-ROM to automated catalogues and the Internet, to downloadable music and books. Their patrons went from mostly older people and families to single men, the unemployed and the homeless as well as those crazy people who snuck in among them.

1

Laser Tag in the Library

To quote Bugs Bunny, "First I was born, which goes without saying." The date was November 4, 1969. I share a birthday with Matthew McConaughey and P. Diddy—or is it Puff Daddy? It was three days before the broadcast premier of *Sesame Street*. According to my sisters the song *Backfield in Motion* was playing on the radio when I was born and according to Wikipedia this was the same year that the books *The Godfather, Slaughterhouse-Five, Papillon* and *The Satanic Bible* were written. My father was a postal worker, my mother a homemaker, and they were 43 and 41 years old when I arrived on the scene. I wasn't exactly planned. My sisters are 15 and 18 years older than me, so they had left home before I was very old. It was a lot like growing up as an only child. Also we lived out in the sticks and there weren't that many children around, so a lot of times I had to entertain myself. No problem there. I had television. I had old horror and sci-fi movies and I had books, both comic and otherwise.

When I was in kindergarten I was reading at a sixth grade level. I don't really remember not being able to read. I could already read the newspaper at that age although I couldn't quite understand it. For example, I read an article on guerrillas fighting in another part of the world. First, I couldn't understand why the person writing the article kept misspelling "gorilla" and second, I really wanted to see those gorillas fighting. I also remember reading an article on the presidential primaries and the author of the column made the statement that Jimmy Carter was a little afraid of the Iowa Caucus. I didn't know what a caucus was but it was kind of a creepy sounding word, caucus, and why was Jimmy Carter afraid of it? All I knew was that we were Republican and my dad seemed happy about the news, so I guess it was good despite the dark sounds of the words used in the article.

But I digress. The idea that I'm trying to get across is that books and reading have always been important to me and important in our household. My parents didn't go to school beyond high school, but they always stressed reading and education. We weren't regular library patrons—the old living out in the sticks thing—but my mother did take me on occasion, and it was a big deal to go. I knew that I would be getting books that I didn't already own.

By the time I started college my interest in books and all things academic had waned. In fact, the first time I attended college my academic performance was far from stellar. It wasn't because I didn't have the brains, it was because it was my first taste of freedom and I put more of my energies into partying and playing music, badly at that. It got to the point that when I was home at break I would watch the mailbox to try and get my grades before my parents did. Is this something that I'm proud of? No, it isn't, in fact my choices when I was getting that first bachelor's degree were some of the worst of my life, and if I could turn back time I would correct it all, but I can't, so I just have to look back on it and try and figure out a way to kick my own butt. At that point I was the first person in my immediate family to attend a four year college, my mother was actually accepted at High Point College (now University) in the forties, but her family couldn't afford to send her. Knowing that, it shows what an immature little brat I was when I attended college the first time and I was lucky they didn't boot my ass out the first semester I was there. I will say that there were other factors that played into my subpar performance that semester, but my introduction to them was my own doing. I have always told people that part of my problem in college was that I had a couple of really good friends who proved to be bad influences. Those friends would be Bud Weiser and Jack Daniels.

> In 1876 the Anheuser-Busch company, an American brewer, began brewing a beer called Budweiser. The word Budweiser is a German word which means someone or something from the city of Ceske Budejovice, or Budweis, which is in Southern Bohemia, the present-day Czech Republic. We're back to Bohemia which, if you'll remember, was where Casanova did his time in the library profession. Beer of this kind had been brewed in Budweis since the 13th century. Jack Daniels is a little newer. The distinctive Tennessee whiskey was the product of its namesake who started his company in 1875. There is an interesting story concerning Jack Daniels the man. It is said that he grew angry one morning in 1911 and kicked his safe because he couldn't get it open. He broke his toe and, as it was not properly cared for, it became infected and, in the ensuing case of blood poisoning, Daniels died. According to experts, however, this was not true.

1. Laser Tag in the Library

The college I was attending at the time was an interesting place. It was a modest, quaint institution and the average class size couldn't have been 20. It was sort of like living in a small town because most people knew each other and the professors and staff knew their students. As I look back on it this was a wonderful thing although, of course, I didn't appreciate it, because it was harder to cut class and engage in such chicanery without the professors noticing. Some would just blow it off because you were supposedly an adult and if you wanted to flunk it was okay with them. Others, however, cared a little more. I had a couple who would call your room if you were absent. I had another corner me when I cut out halfway through a three-hour class and very bluntly expressed her disappointment in my lack of ambition regarding my academics. There was

Me with my sisters, Dale Flinchum (top) and Martha Lewis. There are 15 and 18 years difference between them and me.

a business professor who was also dean of boys; my dad called him "Dean Clower" because of a resemblance to the late comedian Jerry Clower. If a male student happened to be absent from his class, he was known to go to the guy's room—he had a pass key to all the male dorm rooms—walk in unannounced and retrieve said student. I was in his class a couple of times and I never had the guts to skip it because I was afraid he would invade my room and drag me in. I don't know what he would do when a female student missed his class, but he was also known to hand the keys to his Cadillac to another student and have them go retrieve whoever was absent, so maybe he would go that route. The first time I was ever truly chewed out by someone other than my parents was in college about this time. My adviser was a history professor whom we called the "Little Führer" because his area of expertise was the life of Adolf Hitler and he was 5'5" if that. I was in his office for a student conference and he was looking over my grades. There was one grade that we called Lyceum. There were certain events, seminars, plays, concerts, church services and the like, and for four semesters we were required to go to eight a semester. There were a lot more than eight, so it wasn't very hard to go to the allotted amount. Me, being a dumb ass, however, had failed to do this for two semesters when I was signed up for that class, and my adviser's reaction was not pretty. It went something like this.

"Johnny," he said (he was one of the few people who ever called me Johnny and got away with it. I hate being called Johnny). "How the hell do you fail Lyceum!" Then he perused my grades a little further. "I'll be damned if you didn't do it again! You know if you were stupid I wouldn't be so mad but as it is I'd love to wring your fool neck!"

The reason I am mentioning my poor academic performance in college is to illustrate just how important or unimportant the library was to me during my freshman year. It was a large brick building that sat on the opposite side of campus from my dorm and most of the other buildings that I would frequent. It was sort of like Zimbabwe—I knew it was there but I never really wanted to go.

There was a great story concerning our library that I heard through a group of acquaintances. I don't know if it's true or not, but I hope it is. Apparently a few of these "acquaintances" hid in a stall in one of the library bathrooms and, after it had closed, crept out of their hidey hole and started playing laser tag in the book stacks, which were three floors, cramped, dark, and full of little nooks and crannies, perfect for a clandestine war game. Only thing was that one of the combatants ran underneath the stairs and centered his forehead on a metal beam underneath it. The people who were allegedly with him said that he bled like a stuck pig, but after I had started working at the library I asked and nobody had heard of any blood being found in the stacks. Anyway, the wounded gunman was taken to the hospital and stitched up. According to the story, on the way back from the hospital the guys came upon a construction area, and the one with stitches in his head thought that it would be a great idea to borrow a steamroller. He drove it down the four-lane highway that ran in front of our college with his friends leading the way in a car. He parked it somewhere just off campus and left it there. I wasn't able to find any evidence that this occurred other than the "acquaintances" testimony. It may not be true, but again, I hope it is.

I wasn't far into my freshman year before I realized that a little more money coming in would make it possible for more grade-killing fun. Despite the little effort that I had put into my studies, I wasn't afraid of work, so after a quick look over the message board in the student center, I applied for and got a job in the college maintenance department through the work study program, which meant that for every hour I worked a minuscule amount of money would go toward my tuition. The dorm for the freshman boys was called Helms, or HELLms as we

1. Laser Tag in the Library

called it, and it was on the far edge of campus. The maintenance shed, as it was called, was more of a large warehouse and it was right next to my dorm, which was good. Most of my duties involved unpacking boxes and stocking shelves of various items that the maintenance guys would use, cleaning up, your regular grunt work and, sometimes, assisting the maintenance guys when they went out on calls.

The men who worked at maintenance were no-nonsense types. They wore a lot of camouflage with their work clothes and most had beards, sort of like *Duck Dynasty* before there was a *Duck Dynasty*. As far as getting along with them, it varied. Some saw my long hair and looked down on me for it. Some gave me a fair amount of ribbing for it and some were okay. I really didn't work with that many of them on a regular basis. The only person who was a pain in the butt and remained so on a regular basis was a guy named Clark.

My immediate supervisor and his boss were perpetually either absent or holed up in their office with the door shut. This left the student assistants under the charge of Clark, another full-time employee. Clark was a recently graduated alum who had pursued a sociology degree with the understanding that he could move to Miami and become a detective with the Miami PD right off. This position, according to Clark, came with a Ferrari Testarossa just like Sonny Crockett's on *Miami Vice*. I don't know who told him this but none of us were shocked to learn that this didn't work out, and Clark's part-time maintenance job turned into a permanent job and eventually a career. In fact, the last time I was back for homecoming a couple of years ago, Clark went by in a university pickup truck looking a lot like he did the last time I saw him. At the time I worked with him, Clark was jaded and pissed off and spent a great deal of his time at work spouting redneck philosophy and telling all of us that we were wasting our time and our parents' money even pursuing a college degree.

By the time I was a rising sophomore I didn't want to do the maintenance thing anymore, not because the work was that hard, but because if I stayed I thought I would run over Clark with a forklift. One day during summer break I staggered into the house after a long day working as a surveyor's assistant. Eight hours of tracing a property line down the middle of a creek had taught me that I really didn't like hard labor and I was looking for a change.

"Isn't that why I'm going to college?" I asked my mother, and it was at that point that she, right out of the blue, suggested that I get a job at the campus library when I got back to school. She said it would be easier than working at maintenance, so I did because Clark probably wouldn't spend much time in the library. I don't know where Mom got the suggestion. She had definitely pulled it out of nowhere and within a couple of days of returning for my sophomore year,

I walked into the library. I was clad in my usual, heavy metal hair, t-shirt, ripped jeans and Chuck Taylors, dressed for success. I asked who I would talk to concerning a job and I was pointed to an office directly behind the lending desk and a woman named Anne. Anne greeted me with a wide, if not a little yellowed smile, and bid me to sit down in her office, which was extremely cluttered and entirely enclosed in glass. It smelled of cigarette smoke, not "the somebody just smoked in here" cigarette smoke, that wasn't allowed in the library even then, but a "somebody just went outside to smoke and will go outside to smoke when she's done" smell.

"So have you got your class schedule with you, Honey?" she asked. Her voice was a deep smoky growl which bordered on sexy. I gave her my schedule and she disappeared into another room to make a photocopy, sliding her cigarette purse into her pocket for her next planned smoke break. When she came back she slid my schedule back to me and began writing in red pen on another sheet of paper. "I can schedule you Mondays, Wednesdays and Fridays from 3:00–4:30, Tuesday nights 5–9:00, one Saturday and one Sunday a month. That okay?" I said yes and thus I was a librarian. I hadn't even finished filling out the application yet. Anne was one of the many people who I will credit with getting me into my chosen profession. Her job as the supervisor of the student assistants didn't stop with taking our applications. She made out our schedules, which involved not only knowing our class and extracurricular schedules but calling us when we forgot to show up for work, and on a couple of occasions driving students that didn't live on campus home after their shifts were over. Anne knew me as well as the others, knew our backgrounds and took the time to take an interest. Once when I had an important paper due that I

Bright-eyed, full of promise and badly in need of a new suit, with my mom, Molly Farlow.

was hopelessly behind on she let me stay after the library was closed, as were the other computer labs on campus, and waited on me so she could lock up after I was gone.

My favorite Anne moment occurred the morning after Hurricane Hugo hit campus. I got up the next morning and the whole place was a mess of fallen trees and assorted flotsam that had been blown hither and yon by hurricane force winds. There was no electricity on campus, so, not having anything else to do I went to work. I was scheduled so I headed in and found Anne sitting on the steps outside smoking a cigarette.

"Oh honey," she said as I walked up. "What are you doing here? Go on home."

During my last semester in college she took me out to dinner one night at a nice restaurant nearby, which she did for all the assistants. Right after I left Anne took a job elsewhere and left the library. I haven't spoken to her since and I don't know if I thanked her then, but if I didn't I definitely should have.

There are a great many people who are born with the passion to work in a library. I was not one of them. When I was growing up I wanted to be everything from a scientist, to a football player to a para-psychologist—never a librarian.

> Para·psy·chol·o·gy noun \,pa-rə-(,)sī-'kä-lə-jē\ : The branch of psychology that studies psychic phenomena as clairvoyance and telepathy (*Webster's College Dictionary*). One personal note; three of the main characters in the movie *Ghostbusters* were parapsychologists which is where I got the idea. Duke University was apparently a pioneering institution in the field.

I would be lying if I told you that I took my job as seriously as I should have from the start. To begin with, since I was a new employee, my sole duty was shelf reading. That is going from book to book in a particular section of the library shelves and making sure the books are in proper order. As you can imagine, this is a very mundane, very tedious, very necessary duty. In most libraries that I have worked in, it's one of the jobs of part-time employees, but every librarian has done it or should do it. I consider it a rite of passage, sort of like boot camp or getting tazed as a rookie cop to get your tazer. I soon realized the mundane, tedious part. I also realized that, most of the time, nobody would come to check on my progress, so I would regularly show up for work, check in and scan my given section for a few minutes while I listened to the Sex Pistols on my Walkman. Soon the attention span of a gerbil would take over and I would wander through the stacks before I found a book that interested me, and I would begin to shelf read that section, if I didn't just sit down and read through a book. I soon discovered color photography, which included nudes, at TR 675.B65. I also found *Jurassic Park*, the novel, not the movie at PS 3553.R48. My old friend Victor

Frankenstein at PN 1997.F68 F7 and books on heavy metal music, one of my favorite subjects at the time, were at ML 3534.T87. Often a friend would visit me at work and we would hang out, and once a fine, young thing I was seeing stopped by and made my break a little more memorable.

> A professor in graduate school, whom I will mention later, told the class that his favorite Library of Congress subject heading was Gerald Ford-Relations with Boy Scouts. It has to be mine as well.

Luckily for me I worked with a lot of really good, really patient, librarians who did see potential in me, and as the year went on and the next began, I started taking things a lot more seriously. The head of reference, who I will call The Running Man (more on that later), was one such mentor, who was at first a little aloof. He soon proved to be not only a dedicated science fiction fan, but amiable, supportive and encouraging. One afternoon I was at the lending desk, one of the first times, as a matter of fact, being trained in checking someone out, when he ran by like his butt was on fire.

"Is something wrong?" I asked.

"He just does that," I was told, and then he ran by going the other direction. I learned that this was one of The Running Man's many eccentricities. When he went anywhere in the library he would jog rather than walk. After awhile I started jogging along behind him which seemed to generate a great deal of mirth among the other staff. The funniest part of this story is that when I went back to that library after I graduated, I came clean to R. M. about my little prank, and he confessed that he knew I was back there all along and would take an extended route through the library, leading me through the place like some sort of geeky parade.

I did use this particular librarian in probably one of the better pranks that I've ever pulled. One day when another one of the student assistants and I were in a back room hauling off copies of *Modern Medicine Monthly* from 1932 to be discarded, we found the magnetic strips that were put in the spines of the books to make the alarms go off when someone tried to take one out of the building without checking it out. I took one, took it back to my room and slipped it into one of my roommate's notebooks that he always carried in his book bag. I was lucky that I was on duty when my roommate came into the library, studied a while and then went to leave. As soon as he stepped between the two shiny steel corrals, a loud beeping noise sounded, and as my roommate froze where he stood, The Running Man came tearing out of his office, grabbed his backpack, almost dislocating my roommate's shoulder in the process, and proceeded to go through his book bag until he found the metallic strip and removed it. They both were extremely perplexed about how it got there, but I kept my mouth shut and the Case of the Beeping Book has remained a mystery.

Sometime during my junior or senior year the library got a new director. We went from a sweet-natured, grandfatherly, marking time until retirement, spent-most-of-the-time-in-his-office director, to a nice enough, but extremely officious micromanager, and the transition was not without its growing pains. One of the first policies that our new director put in place was that he wrote an official greeting that all employees were to use while answering the phone. Said greeting announced the name of the library, the department and the name of the employee, among other things. It was about a paragraph long and, if memory serves me right it went something like this.

Hello, you have reached the _____ library on the beautiful campus of _____ College. We are located at _____. The campus is located in the Piedmont section of the state of North Carolina, a convenient distance from the majestic mountains and breathtaking coast, which boasts our Outer Banks as well as the Cape Hatteras lighthouse. If you are a visitor to our state you might be interested to know that our state bird is the cardinal, the state flower, the dogwood and the state tree is the pine. If you are lucky you might get to see these beautiful symbols of our state or you might get a chance to pet a plot hound, our state dog, or drink a tall cold glass of our state's beverage, milk. My name is Jon, my student number is 2293, my major is history. I was born in Asheboro, North Carolina and I hope to graduate in the spring of 1992. Our director is _____. He accepted this post on April 8, 1990, at 10:15 a.m. Our hours are Monday through Friday 8:00–10:00, Saturday 8:00–5:00 and Sunday 1:00–9:00. It is now 10:10 a.m. Now how may I help you?

It was typed out and placed beside every phone in the library as a subtle reminder of the proper way to answer the phone. Of course, we didn't go along with that policy right off. It took a couple of times for the Micromanager to call the library and catch us before we relented and promised to deliver the War and Peace version.

One night during the L.A. riots following the Rodney King verdict, I was working a night with M.M. He had heard that there had been trouble on college campuses across the country connected to those riots, and he was worried that there could be some on our campus and that there could be a potential danger to the library.

"I'll be in reference," he said. I was working the lending desk. "If there's any trouble I want you to call me. The code word is Zorro." Let me reiterate that. "The code word is Zorro." Not a word that you might say from time to time like "strawberry" or "clothes dryer." No, Zorro, and this made the night ripe for a little

Scott, me and the Rabbi at Scott's 40th.

fun. A friend and hall mate of mine we called the Rabbi, because of a resemblance to your stereotypical Jewish rabbi, was assisting in the AV room and, since it was slow, he spent most of the time hanging out at lending. Every time the director would come by we would work the word "Zorro" into our conversation and say it loud. The director would stop and look around really quickly like he was expecting someone to jump him from any direction. I think we had him as nervous as a long tailed cat, and I'm sure he was glad when the night was over.

Speaking of the Rabbi, one night after the library closed he climbed in through a conveniently unlocked window. When the library was opened the morning after his visit you might find a stapler with a label on it that said "stapler." You might find a book with a label that said "book." You might find a pencil with a label that said, you guessed it, "pencil." We found a label on a wall that said "wall." A label beside a tool that was unique to library work said "thing" and a label on a wall with an arrow pointing toward another label said "label." I thought it was hilarious. Of course, I knew who had done it but I didn't tell anybody. I think that I was the only one who worked at the library who appreciated the humor. I know that M.M. didn't because he called the police. At the time the town where our college was located was so small that the town police and the campus police were one and the same. The chief was a man named Rufus who knew the Rabbi as well as his proclivity for practical jokes.

"Just stay away from the library after it's closed," he said with a grin. "Oh I'm sorry." He gave the Rabbi a knowing wink. "Tell whoever left the notes to stay away from the library after it's closed."

When I started college I was a music business major because I wanted to start a rock band and see the world. This was many years before I came to the conclusion that I have no musical talent. It wasn't until I was most of my way through my first bachelor's degree, which I had switched to history, that I, with the encouragement of the staff I worked with, started looking at being a librarian as a career. I started at the library because it was easier than maintenance and I needed the money. It was in the three years that I worked at the college library that I realized libraries' importance and chose the library as my career.

2

Library 101

If you look back at the history of libraries themselves, you can see that they came to be in much the same way that I came to work in them. They came to be out of necessity, not because someone said to themselves, "Son of a gun I think I'll start a library." This fact, that libraries rose out of necessity, and very early in human history, is a testament to the fact that they are, in some form or other, important to a developed society.

Many experts believe that it was the Sumerians who invented writing by developing cuneiform, a wedge shaped script, written into clay with styluses made of reeds. They are also credited with inventing graffiti when someone wrote, "Here I sit broken hearted" on the wall of a temple bathroom. The Sumerian economy revolved around grain production, and elaborate records were kept, tracking harvests and cultivation. Soon other records were added to them, such as information on manufacturing, the owning of land and other economic records, then temple records and religious documents and hymns, as well as literature of the other Mesopotamian languages such as Assyrian, Akkadian, Ugaritic and Aramaic. The clay tablets that these documents were written on were durable, but they took up a lot of space and were kept in temples and stored in wooden, reed or brick receptacles. The contents of these containers were labeled. There was also a catalog of sorts, called the Hammurabi Decimal System, just kidding, which recorded the titles and the number of the tablets that made up that title. Many times they were stored in rooms that could only be entered via ladder. One true fact that most modern librarians can identify with was that soon after these early libraries were created, space became an issue and often times tablets were set on floors, in hallways and even in doorways.

Four centuries after the Sumerian libraries slipped beneath the sand, a flamboyant Greek hotshot, named Alexander, swept across the continent and, in 331 BC decided to build an entire city in Egypt on the shore of the Mediterranean. It would be called Alexandria, and legend has it that he marked the perimeter of the future city with flour. (I would expect that this is a story that is more tall tale than fact.) Alexander would not live to see Alexandria's glory, but his former general Ptolemy I, who, according to the Oliver Stone movie *Alexander* looked a lot like Anthony Hopkins, would make it the capital of the Ptolemaic Dynasty.

> The Gordian Knot was so complicated and hard to get loose that it was said that whoever could untie it would rule the world. According to legend, when it was presented to Alexander, he cut through it with his sword and then untied it.

The Royal Library of Alexandria came into existence sometime between 323 and 246 BC. The library was part of the museum of Alexandria and a symbol of the glory of Egypt, as well as one of the wonders of the ancient world. Although the exact size of the collection housed at Alexandria is unknown, some experts estimate that it was between 650,000 and 1,000,000 scrolls. Preeminent scholars were invited to the library by the royal family where they would live and eat together. They would be given an extraordinary amount of freedom at the library to translate and take down the world's documents onto papyrus scrolls to become part of the library's collection. Did the Ptolemys go to these lengths just because they were that obsessed with the accumulation and extension of knowledge? Partially, but they also realized the military strategy of hording knowledge. They even went so far as to confiscate the materials of visitors to the city and have them copied. Sometimes both the copies and the originals were added to the collection of the library.

There is no physical evidence to lend much to the details of the Library of Alexandria. We don't know how the scrolls were stored, but we do know that the scrolls were marked with tags bearing the author and title of the work. They were then attached to an umbilicus which was the wooden peg the scroll was wrapped around. The fact that the works at this library were on scrolls instead of tablets can give a hint about how the library's shelves might have looked. They would most likely be in piles rather than stacks or standing up on shelves. If a patron were to need a particular scroll, they or the librarian may have to shift a great deal to get access to it. Because of the rather precarious way the scrolls were grouped, the order would be generalized as opposed to the exact order that we have today.

There has been a rumor through the ages that during the Muslim conquest of Egypt in 641 AD, the Arab general 'Amr ibn al-Āṣ invaded and sought the advice of the Caliph Omar as to what to do "with the books of the infidels." The answer was sent back from Medina to see if they agreed with the Koran. If they did, they were unnecessary; if they didn't, they were wicked. The fires of the four thousand bath houses of Alexandria were supposedly fueled for six months on the materials taken out of the great library. Alas, this is just a rumor and the collapse of the library at Alexandria was collective rather than one that came about because of one catastrophic event.

The fact that these scrolls were written on papyrus as opposed to clay tablets, like in Sumeria, was the main reason that the Library of Alexandria seemed to attract lit matches. In Greek historian Plutarch's *Parallel Lives*, he describes a battle in the siege of the city in 48 BC where, during a skirmish between Julius Caesar and Ptolemy XIII ol' Julie was forced to burn his own ships and accidentally set fire to the Royal Library, incinerating some 400,000 scrolls. The library also burned during the 270s during an attack by the Roman emperor Aurelian.

Another rumor that rose not long afterward, and had a large hand in the demise of the Library of Alexandria, was that the Christians of the day, who had long been persecuted, now sought revenge on the culture that had put its boot on their necks for so long. The pagan culture that had nurtured science and literature was shoved aside by religious fanatics who came to dominate the city of Alexandria and lynched the philosopher and mathematician Hypatia in 415. Shortly before that, in 391, the Bishop Theophilus led a mob to set fire to the library once again.

Coinciding with Theophilus's attack, the library no longer had the same cultural and scholarly importance that it once had, as Ptolemy XIII had begun to expel many of the intellectuals, philosophers and artists who had opposed him earlier in his reign. After the Romans conquered Egypt the library continued to operate, but it was no longer the intellectual paragon—that title now belonged to Rome. That being said, it doesn't look like there was enough left of the library by the time 'Amr ibn al-Āṣ arrived to furnish one bathhouse, much less a city full. It can be said that strife, war and ignorance were what swept away the glory that was once the Library of Alexandria. Fire is bad, invading armies horrible, but what intellectual institution can stand up against such a tidal wave of stupidity?

I mentioned the Romans. The Roman Empire was a very public society. They socialized in public, they bathed in public, probably had sex in public, and committed sanctioned murder in front of thousands. Because of this it shouldn't be surprising that they had public libraries of a sort. Actually the first libraries in Rome were private, and if you know anything about how the Roman Empire operated you won't be shocked to know that some of these libraries were stocked with materials claimed as war booty and brought back to Rome by the empire's armies. No matter how they were collected, libraries were the property of the social elite and materials were shared with the owner's friends and peers. A public library was the idea of Julius Caesar, you remember him, the genius who accidentally burned down a large chunk of the Library of Alexandria? Well, apparently the library had made a large enough impact that Caesar wanted Rome to have a large library for use by his citizens. Alas, Julius Caesar would not see this library built before he ran afoul of Brutus's blade, but nevertheless, the library would be brought into existence five years after Julie's death. It should be said that the first libraries were not libraries as we think of them today. They were books stored on shelves located in warehouses or similar buildings and patrons would take them outside to read them. One aspect of Roman libraries was designed at the beginning and would remain throughout their existence. That is Roman libraries, no matter the location, were separated into two sections; one for Greek and one for Latin. The reason for the Latin section should be obvious, as that was the language of the Roman Empire. The reason for a Greek section is that the Hellenistic tradition was still very strong. Being the stud that he was, Alexander the Great's shadow was long; he influenced art, architecture, city planning and, in this way, libraries. Or then again maybe Romans just didn't like Greeks and wanted them in another part of the library. You see, segregation didn't start in the South.

Augustus followed Caesar and would become Rome's first true emperor. He liked to boast that he found Rome brick and left it marble. Included in his plans to bring grandeur to the city was a library. He built a library adjacent to the temple of Apollo and then another nearby dedicated to his sister, Octavia. The first had the customary two reading rooms for the two languages, Greek and Latin. Most of the materials were on scrolls which were on shelves. After Augustus the construction of a library became the in-project for the emperors that came after him, almost like politicians and their pet projects. Trajan's library was a massive building that had the two sections facing each other and a massive column dedicated to the man himself in the middle. Tiberius built a library next to his palace, Vespasian built another library in Rome next to the Forum that bore his name and Tiberius followed suit in the same city. By the time Constantine split the empire in twain, Rome was home to 28 public libraries. The majority of these institutions were in either public baths or gymnasiums. The baths were the social centers of the day and the libraries were carefully laid out so that the scrolls were far enough away from the water so that the ultra absorbent papyrus wouldn't be damaged by the moisture. These scrolls were for lending and materials could be removed from the premises and taken home. The gymnasiums were not like our gymnasiums of today with locker rooms, basketball courts and sweaty guys yelling: "Dude!" The gymnasiums that I am speaking of were more like colleges or universities. They were gathering places for students, complete with a library. The people of

Cos started a public library. The building and 100 scrolls were donated by two wealthy citizens, Diocles and his son Apollodorus. Other citizens were expected to provide 150 scrolls, or if they were lacking in this area, they were taxed 200 drachmas. The fact that the public was charged with assisting in the funding and maintenance of the library fully makes it a modern type of public library.

As Rome began to fade from prominence and collapse into civil war, personal libraries were confiscated or burned by the people on the other side of the political fence. When Constantine transferred the capital to Constantinople, Rome's decay was accelerated and libraries began closing up one after the other. In a great deal of the old Roman cities the libraries that were left were torn down, burned or left to blow away in the wind.

During the Middle Ages libraries, such as they were, were centered around monasteries. The Rule of St. Benedict called for the reading of "Christian literature" as a part of monastic life, along with being quiet and cutting their hair with their scalp showing in the middle and, no, this Christian literature had nothing to do with the *Left Behind* series. Stipulations called for the monastery to possess at least one book for each of its members. Each monk was to receive one book and read it straight through. In addition to books of psalms, hymnals, commentaries and biographies of the saints, there were textbooks used in the classrooms and legal, medical and technical books used by the higher-ups. In addition to reading the books themselves, books were actually read out loud while the monks took their meals.

It was during this period that Christian scholars introduced the codex or the bound book, which is the format we largely use today, and no folks, the e-reader hasn't come close to replacing it yet. Christians had picked up the codex in Palestine, Egypt and Greece where it was based on portfolios of ivory or wood carried there. For libraries, the codex was no more resistant to decay, but they were easier to read, easier to store and required less repair.

The men who came to these monasteries were not slaves or peasants. More often than not they came from aristocratic families and brought the love of reading with them when they came, as well as books of a more secular bent. The collections of the monasteries grew to be quite vast with well developed collections encompassing many different subjects and containing books that could be beautiful and expensive. Regardless, books were sometimes lent out to clergy and noblemen. Commoners could take out books for religious reading but they had to leave a book of theirs as collateral. A record was made when the book was taken out and when it was brought back. Still this service was not akin to public libraries as we would recognize them in the modern era. It was provided as a favor and not a right.

These holy men who presided over these collections were not called librarians, but that is exactly what they were. At the time, these monastic libraries were the few repositories of written knowledge. In fact, a huge majority of the knowledge that survived through the Dark Ages into the Renaissance was saved and studied by holy men. This is unusual when you think that the Middle Ages were trademarked by rampant religiosity and monks and holy men are not known for cultivating knowledge—religious or otherwise—even though they played a major role in it.

As the Middle Ages passed, universities were founded in the larger cities and information became a little more widespread. As the Renaissance started and the printing press was developed, knowledge became even more accessible and libraries multiplied and grew. Libraries became a status symbol among the hoity toity of the day and those collections first put together by the social elite formed the basis of many great libraries in Europe, such as France's Bibliothèque Nationale.

While Europe was still in the full grip of the Dark Ages, culture and learning moved east into the Orient and the Middle East. As culture and education flourished, libraries grew along with them, although they would be private rather than open to what we would call the general public.

The Chinese invented writing so that they could keep a record of religious ceremonies. When a sacrifice was made to the gods, a record of it was made and written on ox bones or tortoise shells. On some rare occasions they were hidden in little cookies. It was in the Chou Dynasty that correspondence between different governments and government agencies grew exponentially and this led to the creation of court archives. These libraries were extremely important to court life. So important, in fact, that Fred Lerner mentions in his book, *The Story of Libraries*, that the resignation of a royal archivist was worthy of being mentioned in court records. Some people from the upper class were trained from birth to become civil servants and they studied not only the art of war but the ancient classics, which came into being between 551 and 479 BC and were credited to the philosopher who we in the Western world call Confucius, and were called the Five Classics. Some of the aristocrats of this day owned huge book collections and during the Chou Dynasty evolved into libraries. The ministers of religion were in charge of the materials that recorded rites and ceremonies. The minister of education was put in charge of calendars which recorded the planting of crops by kingdom's farmers.

The Chou Dynasty gave way to the Ch'in Dynasty of 221 BC and they took a slightly different view of learning and reading. They sought a more centralized government, revamped the written language and went all *Fahrenheit 451* trying to burn all the materials that they did not agree with. As is often the case when fascists start burning books, this wasn't the first nor the last time many private libraries were rescued and hidden, which is how the modern world still has access to the Five Classics of Confucius. When the Han Dynasty rose in 206 BC, the Five Classics, as well as libraries, enjoyed a renaissance of sorts. The emperor put together a committee of scholars to interpret the classics. They also put together a training school to educate candidates for high office, which looking at the type of person the U.S. always seems to elect, I think this is a wonderful idea. An imperial library was established and one of its main purposes was to collect officially sanctioned copies of the classics. Let me say that again, *officially sanctioned* copies of the classics—that is, the version with Big Brother's stamp of approval—and distribute them throughout the Han empire.

One of the Han emperors, Wu Ti, who reigned from 140 to 87 BC, had officials in his cabinet whose job it was to transcribe various classics that would be stored at the imperial library. Agents for the emperor scoured the countryside in search of books to serve this purpose and a general reward was offered to anyone who loaned the emperor's officials a written work to be copied and taken to the library. One of the other Han emperors, Ch'eng ti, 33 to 7 BC, appointed royal adviser, Liu Hsiang, to revise the content of the library. I guess we would call it weeding if it were to go on these days. Hsiang developed a catalog of the collection, the first in that part of the world. His son, Liu Hsin, devised a book to classify the books in the collection. The books were divided into one of seven categories: General, The Classics, Philosophy, Poetry, Military Science, Astronomy and Mathematics and Divination, and Medicine and Trades. Close to the end of the Han Dynasty the classics of Confucius were carved into a large stone situated on the campus of the Imperial University. It took 46 stones to contain the more than 200,000 characters, and university patrons would bring moistened paper and make rubbings of the classics off the stones. This provided a constant supply of the classics, and if the patron was one of those people who likes the librarian to do everything for them, rubbings could be made by library officials for a fee.

Over the following decades dynasties came and went, and when a new one came it was not unusual for the content of the libraries to sustain heavy losses. Then the next dynasty would come along and try to recreate the classics which may or may not be destroyed themselves when the next dynasty rose to power. The Imperial Library, however, stayed in operation, although it declined dramatically. There was a period of 400 years between the Han and Sui dynasties where the country was divided into numerous hostile and often warring territories. When the Sui took over in 581, the powers that be sought to justify their rule and wanted to use the works of Confucius for this purpose—sort of like modern politicians and the Bible—and both groups were probably just as earnest in their interest of either work. The Sui and their successors, the Tang, sought to bring the library back to its former glory and, like the Han, sent officials out into the country to borrow rare books from the libraries of private citizens. A bolt of silk was given to each person who loaned a book for copy.

One institution that came about during the Tang Dynasty was the history department which, as the name implies, was commissioned to put together the histories of the Dynasty—which had formerly fallen upon the staff of the library—as well as the obituaries of former emperors and high ranking officials of state. The reason for the compilation of such information went beyond scholarly. It served a political purpose as well, since they, like the Sui, sought to use this information to validate the legitimacy of their rule.

The main purpose of the Imperial Library during the Tang Dynasty was to collect and catalog the best of Chinese literature. About this time, earlier library catalogs were used as checklists of works to be located, copied and kept at the library. Your work being accepted at the Imperial Library and the accompanying seal of approval that library officials would put on said works was highly sought after. A talent for composing prose was an important talent and the best works were compiled in large encyclopedias, sort of like those *Best of the Year* compilations of short stories these days, the one that every library has several years worth of in its collection and are never checked out. Earlier works were compiled in similar compilations to inspire current writers.

During the Tang years, which were largely peaceful, literacy increased, as did the production of books and the holdings of private collectors grew quite large. In the eighth century, some of these collections rivaled the Imperial Library, which had grown quite massive in its own right. In AD 721 the holdings of the Imperial Library, which was then located in Chang'an, numbered 3,060 titles and 51,952 short stories, or chuanqui as they were known. Ten years later the collection had grown to 89,000 chuanqui and this did not include the holdings of the library in the eastern capital of Luoyang.

In the middle of the eighth century the library suffered substantial damage during the rebellion of General An Lu-shan and, after that the Tang Dynasty began losing power. After its fall the country saw a return to the revolving door—destroy the collection and then build it back again—of previous dynasties. By the time the capital was moved from Chang'an to Luoyang the collection of the library had fallen to ten thousand chuanqui. Then, under the Sung, who came to power in the later part of the tenth century, an interest in scholarship was again revived and wood block printing was introduced. Through this medium the classics of Confucius, a 130-volume edition, as well as other works, were mass produced and distributed throughout the country. Once again the holdings of libraries both official and private began to rebound. However the Imperial Library continued to fade from existence.

> The world's earliest surviving book on the craft of librarianship is *Lin-t'ai ku-shih* (A tale of the national library), written by Ch'eng Chu. Based on a study of earlier Chinese libraries, it was written to encourage the reestablishment of an imperial library after the destruction unleashed by the invasion of the Jurched hordes from Manchuria. Ch'eng argued that such a library was essential to good government. "It offered the aspirants to the civil service the books that they must read to prepare for selective service examination, and allowed the experiences for earlier rulers and the wisdom of former sages to be applied to contemporary issues. Ch'eng Chu also emphasized that the library would be invaluable for scholarly editors, historians and encyclopedists. In addition to listing the purposes served by a national library, *Lin-t'ai ku-shih* explained the technical aspects of library work—the processes of acquisitions, cataloging, classification, and circulation—as well as the selection and management of library staff and the design of a building fit to house the national library [Lerner p. 59].

Chu's book helped to persuade those in power to reinstate the Imperial Library and massive donations were made by private collectors who were in turn compensated with money, silks and the opportunities to make nominations to civil service positions.

As the centuries passed the same routine seemed to play itself out as more dynasties came and went and each sought to make its mark on the history of China and to develop the literary and library aspects of their culture. The Ch'ing emperor, Ch'ien-lung (1736–1795) pulled together a group of eminent scholars to compile what was known as Ssu-k'u ch'uan-shu or *Complete Library of the Four Treasures*. The Imperial Library and other private collections were examined and certain works were compiled into uniform volumes. The entire project took almost twenty years and employed 15,000 scholars. What came of this Herculean task were seven copies containing thirty-six thousand volumes, and that was just the index, just kidding, but it's hard to imagine a book that long that isn't connected to *Game of Thrones*. This project was not without its selfish and somewhat heinous intentions. The same scholars who looked for works to be rewritten also looked for works that might fall under Imperial disfavor. Those works were burned. In a single day in 1781, 52,840 woodblocks that were used to print these works were broken up and used for firewood.

In the seventh century, when the Muslim armies rode out of the desert, they had no literature aside from the Koran. What separated these armies from a lot of others is that they actually held a certain amount of respect for the cultures of the civilizations they conquered. The Muslim poet, Al-Mutanabi once stated:

"the most honorable seat in this world is in the saddle of a horse and the best companion will always be a book."

The earliest Muslim books were done on papyrus, parchment or bark. Unlike the scrolls of the Chinese or the Sumerians they were done in a codex format, the same form used by their Christian neighbors. Muslim culture placed a lot of emphasis on reading the Koran and had a lot of respect for learning. Their beliefs also steered artists away from graven images, as well as such artistic forms as painting and sculpture, and toward printing, calligraphy and architecture. Also there were paper mills in Baghdad by 794 and a flourishing paper industry in Egypt. This lowered the price of printing books and bookstores flourished in every city in the Muslim world.

The Abbasid caliphate al-Ma'mun who ruled from 813 to 833 AD, founded the House of Wisdom in his capital city of Baghdad. It was modeled after the Library of Alexandria and it was the center for learning, having books that were translated from Greek and Persian among other languages. Under other rulers books were brought back from raids on such civilizations as the Byzantine Empire. Al-Ma'mun preferred a more warm and fuzzy approach to acquiring works for his library. He actually dispatched ambassadors to other rulers such as Emperor Leo V the Armenian and was able to put together a collection covering such subjects as music, philosophy, mathematics, science and medicine.

By the tenth century the first public libraries in the Muslim world began to appear. By then Islamic law had begun to include the concept of charitable law and eventually it was expanded to include funds for public libraries. The waqf, or endowment, used to start libraries was an actual body of Islamic law. There were three requirements to achieve this allotted funding. One, the presentation to a religious tribunal a list of works to be contained there and recorded in its register; second, the attestation of qualified witnesses; and third, a plate inside each book telling of the source of the endowment.

These libraries were called the Dar al-Ilm, or hall of science, and were created to instruct the public in the doctrines of a specific Islamic sect. Scholars were maintained at the library for the instruction of the patrons and as the years passed and the Islamic world expanded and touched almost every civilization, there was ample opportunity for the acquisition of science, literature and other knowledge from other peoples.

The first Dar al-Ilm was located in Mosul and it opened at the very beginning of the tenth century. All people were welcome and foreign scholars were brought in to deliver lectures. These scholars were compensated with ink and paper as well as food and drink. A similar institution was started by Sabur ibn Ardashir in Baghdad around 996. It contained 10,400 volumes including 100 Korans. This

Dar al-Ilm was one of the city's cultural centers and was frequented by poets, scholars and musicians. Many works were donated to this library but the institution was very exclusive and not all works were accepted.

Another Muslim city which became a cultural hub for the Muslim world was the Spanish city of Cordova, some 25 years after Muslims invaded Spain in AD 710. The university located there was known as a center for Islamic studies, mathematics, astronomy and medicine. The city was the second largest, after Constantinople, on the continent. Its book bazaar and 70 libraries attracted scholars of all kinds from all corners of the world. The royal library there was founded by Muhammed I (852–886) and was expanded by Al-Hakam II (961–976). Al-Hakam sent agents to Alexandria, Baghdad and Damascus with instructions to buy or copy certain manuscripts. He also employed copyists and book binders with as many as 500 people on his payroll. The library quickly grew to 400,000 volumes and it took 44 large volumes to list all the materials contained there, and whenever the library had to move locations it would take six months to move everything. Al-Hakam so liked books and learning that libraries and private collections sprouted up all over the country under his control, and the scholarship of Al-Hakam II was so great that books with his notes in the margin were judged to be more valuable.

In the Muslim world libraries became great status symbols to any caliph, so anyone who rose to prominence would build and maintain them. Before the Mongol invasion of the mid–13th century there were 36 libraries in Baghdad alone, 20 of which were actual public libraries. Other libraries existed in mosques. Some collectors did not have the resources to actually endow a gift on public libraries but still wanted to make their books available to those who wished to use them, so books were left at mosques because they were sure to be where people could get them to borrow. The Grand Mosque of Damascus contained several collections which numbered over 5,000 volumes. These libraries were very similar to the ones located in medieval monasteries, as they were more instructional rather than research based, and ultimately they were there to serve the mosque in which they were located.

In these libraries the books were often stored in very ornate cabinets which were in turn separated into cubby holes. The books were arranged in the order they were listed in the library's inventory, with Korans stored separately, often on a higher level than the other books. A subject classification was maintained but it was oftentimes different with every collection that was donated to the library. Books were kept off the floor to protect against humidity and stored in cabinets which were glassed in to guard against dust and insects. When a patron came to "check out" a book from an Islamic library of this type, he might request a specific book or that the library's catalog be brought to him. Some libraries did lend out their books, but others would simply provide the patron with paper and ink to take notes. If he wanted to copy the entire book, with the library's permission, he would have to bring his own materials.

Like the other libraries mentioned already, the Islamic libraries were far from permanent. In fact they suffered much the same fate as the libraries of China. Caliphates, or Islamic states, came and went, and not all of them were sympathetic to the library. To some they were just piles of paper. In 1031 when Umayyad was toppled in Spain, the library was dispersed among a handful of smaller monarchs. In 1175 when Saladin conquered Egypt, he allowed his followers to pick through the library and take what they wanted. In the 12th century Islamic libraries were destroyed by crusaders. When the Muslim Caliphates on the Iberian peninsula were taken down in the period known as the Reconquista, the Cardinal Francisco Ximénez de Cisneros organized a purge of Muslim books. Eighty thousand were purged in 1499 alone and fewer than 2,000 books survived. When the Mongols attacked Muslim lands in the 13th century they destroyed some of the great cities of Asia, Baghdad in 1258. In one week 36 of the city's public libraries were destroyed and only about 1 in 1,000 books survived the Mongol raids where beautiful manuscripts with exquisite calligraphy were burned for fuel and finely decorated leather bindings were worn as shoes.

> As someone who has checked in many a book over the years, it doesn't surprise me one bit that sometime in the history of the human race someone has worn books as shoes. Let's face it, people really aren't that careful with them whether they own them or borrow them from the library. We put them under the short leg of the kitchen table, throw them at our spouses, kids and pets and use them to start campfires. Hardly a week goes by that we don't get a book in that has a brand new coffee ring tattoo, or crayon drawings on the back cover, some x-rated, or a wet sucker stuck in between pages 234 and 235. I have personally checked books in with wax in and on them and unidentified bodily fluids smeared throughout. Some were being donated as gifts and as soon as someone opened the covers, silverfish and cockroaches went in every direction. In the last library I worked in, I think that the lending staff sort of kept a mental list of all the strange things that had been found in library books when they were checked back in. One day they called me over and made it a point of showing me a snapshot that they had found in a novel. It was of a young lady, a great deal younger than me, but not a child by any stretch of the imagination. She was wearing some kind of halter top and a pair of cut off Daisy Dukes. She was reclining very seductively on your average Naugahyde

couch in a somewhat lacking attempt to look like a *Playboy* centerfold. I don't know who this picture was meant for but I doubt it was for me or anybody else at the library. I've always wondered whether or not she ever remembered the picture, figured out where she had left it and who might be looking at it. The grossest thing that I have found in a book personally, was one I had received from another library via interlibrary loan. This book was filled with human hair! The book was *North Dallas Forty* by Peter Gent which is a very bare-chested, manly, testosterone-ridden novel but I didn't really expect it to grow hair!

Here in our modern era these problems extend to other types of materials. When I was still working at my hometown library, one of my duties was to manage the AV collection. These duties involved not only purchasing the DVDs, audiobooks and other such resources, but the maintenance and upkeep of them. One Saturday we received a call from a small furniture store just a couple of blocks from the library. The gentleman on the phone said that his mother had purchased some of our DVDs from a young man who had been in their store the day before. She had not realized that they were library property despite the barcode on the back, and the multiple stamps on the cover and the disc that declared it property of the library. I thanked the man and headed over to the store on my lunch break with some money from the petty cash box, with the director's permission. I thought that it would be a nice gesture to offer to buy back the DVDs. When I got to the store a couple of the man's kids were watching one of our movies, *The Searchers*, with John Wayne. I talked to the man and thanked him for helping us get our property back, but when I offered to pay his mother back for the DVDs he said for me not to worry with it.

"She bought them," he said rather curtly. "It's her problem." When I got back to the library we were able to find out that the movies were checked out by an older lady who told us that she was almost positive that it was her son who sold them and she was pretty sure that he sold them for drugs.

The point that I'm trying to make is that as long as there have been libraries and books, including scrolls, tablets and the other materials that preceded it, then patrons have been abusing them. In the early days they were burning them, wearing them for shoes or drying off in the bathhouses with them. Today we are just as destructive, just a little less blatant about our abuse, or maybe we're just clueless.

So far in this chapter I have covered hundreds of years and a lot of libraries. Still we haven't yet reached what we here in our modern era would call a public library. True, some shared a quality or two with those institutions, open to the general public, public funded, the required number of shush signs, bad-tempered staff members, etc. Some were even called "public libraries" or some version of those two words, but the true-blue, genuine article didn't come along until much later.

In his book *Foundations of Library and Information Science*, Richard E. Rubin gives the following criteria for a library to be considered a public one.

1. Supported by taxes. They are usually supported by local taxes. Before the 19th century the idea of public support through taxation is rare.
2. Governed by a board. This board is specifically formed to work in the public interest.
3. Open to all. A basic tenant to all public libraries is that it is open to all members of the community.
4. Its use is voluntary. People do not have to come; the use of the library is completely up to them.
5. Established by state law. "This point is not generally well understood. During the early development of libraries, serious questions arose concerning whether a town could create a public institution and tax its citizens for its maintenance without state approval. As a consequence a key aspect of the creation of public libraries was the passage of 'enabling legislation' on the part of the states that permitted the creation of public libraries on a local level" (Rubin, p. 285).
6. Provides services without charge to the user. Yes, some libraries charge small fees for such services as copies and interlibrary loans, but most services are free of charge and there is considerable support among librarians for those services to remain free.

Libraries that fit these guidelines didn't just crop up in America, or anywhere else for that matter. When they did make their emergence they did so gradually as great things often do.

Private libraries existed in America from colonial times in the households of such people as doctors and ministers, and sometimes these collections—which might number from a few dozen to a few hundred—were donated to churches and were opened to the public. The bad thing about these collections was that they were poorly maintained and would vanish in a short amount of time.

Colleges and universities had private libraries in America as early as 1638 when John Harvard donated around 200 books and an endowment to some college that would go on and make a respectable name for itself. The typical college library was quite small and received little support from administration or faculty. Some faculty member, probably the low guy on the totem pole, was tapped to supervise the library. He received no compensation so this was not a highly sought after position.

As far as public libraries, the modern system evolved from three trends. The first is the so-called "social library" invented by Benjamin Franklin who had a library of 4,000 books at the time of his death. In 1731 he started his own subscription library as a way of sharing books among associates who belonged to a literary society. Books could only be borrowed by members of the society and to become part of it one had only to buy stock in the society. Once this idea took hold, libraries of this type became very popular. Basically these were the large collections of a private citizen who sold access to their library for a small fee. Soon variants on this one idea cropped up. One was the Athenaeum which was a social library focused on scholarly magazines and newspapers and reserved for the upper crust. It was basically a country club with books and a high price tag to keep out the riff raff. Another play on the social library was the mercantile library. These were founded by the aforementioned upper crust to help educate the uneducated masses, namely young men, to promote orderly and virtuous habits as well as the desire for knowledge and scientific skill. A lot of times this was from a benevolent factory owner for their employees, factory workers and mercantile clerks.

The next trend to push libraries toward being true public libraries was what would be known as circulating libraries which saw their birth at about the same time as the social libraries. These were oftentimes housed in print shops and bookstores and rented out books including the most popular fiction. The first one was possibly opened in 1762 and lasted only two years.

Later on school districts were expected to have books for their students. The thing was they were at the mercy of those who donated materials, whether they jived with what was being taught at their particular school or not. School libraries were pushed for in the 1830s and those who wanted them were asking several basic questions. When we educate our children what do they have to read? Educators and politicians looked to those school libraries to provide books for adults in their district as well as children.

The first library to combine all of those concepts, sharing quality books from social libraries, introducing popular materials from circulating libraries and the idea of public funding from the school libraries, was thought to be the glorious accident that was the town library of Peterborough, New Hampshire which first saw the light of day in 1833. New Hampshire had started collecting taxes to start a state college, but that effort went the way of all flesh and the allotted money was disbursed among various towns to support education. Peterborough decided to use some of that money to start a public library.

2. Library 101

The Boston Public Library opened in 1854, and is usually considered the first real public library; that is intentionally founded, not a happy accident like the Peterborough Library. Its mission statement says:

1. There's a close linkage between knowledge and right thinking.
2. The future of democracy is contingent on an educated citizenry.
3. There's a strong correlation between the public library movement and public education; and
4. Every citizen has the right of free access to community owned resources.

"The creation of the Boston Public Library can be seen in at least two lights: first, as a natural outgrowth of prevailing social attitudes and developments at work by the mid–19th century; and second, as the result of efforts by a group of specific individuals who, for whatever reason, concluded that a public library was an appropriate institution for the citizens of Boston.

"Not only the emergence of the Boston Public Library, but that of public libraries in general, can be seen as a natural outgrowth of other institutional developments of the period. As cities matured and prospered economically their political and bureaucratic structure also matured. Boston was typical of a prospering and stable urban environment, where wealth had accumulated both generally and among specific individuals. In such sophisticated urban settings, it was not uncommon to have a highly developed urban infrastructure provide basic structure such as water, sanitation, public health, fire, water and education. As a result, when the issue was first raised in Boston, it was perceived from an administrative point of view as a logical extension of city services." (Rubin p. 286) In addition there was a growing belief at the time that Boston Public first came into being so that social institutions could uplift and improve people. The library was included in this group of institutions. The Grand Poobah of libraries himself, Melville Dewey, stated that public education was divided into two parts, the free school and the free public library. He saw the library as a school and the librarian as a teacher. Many librarians of the era saw themselves as agents who could help to spearhead social improvements.

In my research I did find mention of an issue which, I feel, is still prevalent and still one that greatly interests me. We have said a lot in these last few sentences that a motivating factor in the establishing of a great many libraries was to benefit the public, or a smaller section thereof. If the library is to bring culture and education to its patrons, what about entertainment? Is the library supposed to bring amusement to him as well as enlightenment? The director of the library where I once worked quoted me the mission statement of our library. "The library is to meet the educational and entertainment needs of the citizens of _____

County." From what I've been able to read, this has been a point of contention for librarians. Boston librarian Charles Ticknor felt that a collection of popular works should be kept along with scholarly works to advocate a love of reading. Others, however, expressed a concern over providing popular novels to the public because, not that they would basically be putting crappy books into the collection, but because some felt that the library would be contributing to the moral decline of its patrons. It was suggested by some that too much popular fiction could even contribute to insanity! Did the library want to have such materials in the library knowing what potential risks that the patrons were being exposed to? Most librarians rightfully felt that if they had a collection of popular literature, that less educated readers might come into the library who would otherwise not darken the door. Once in, maybe they would be exposed to more quality literature. Librarians realized that if they wanted people to come into the library they would need popular fiction. When we say that these collections were stocked with popular literature, we do not mean that they actually included dime novels or pulp magazines. Instead they included works by Flaubert, Zola, Fielding and Balzac. These novels were scandalous in the day, but still pretty high quality literature. You have to think that if people pitched that much of a fit over Flaubert or Fielding, what would they have thought of *Fifty Shades of Grey*?

Another issue would confront libraries up until just a few years ago, and that issue concerned not what they would keep on their shelves but who they would truthfully serve. During the 19th century the United States experienced a huge influx of immigrants, mainly into the larger cities. There were concerns over educational institutions improving society and advancing the democratic tradition. For some this meant that immigrants had to quickly be assimilated into American society. Librarians were to provide the fuel for the fires under the American melting pot. Who better than librarians to provide the necessary material to the necessary people? Many librarians took their role in this process very seriously, but for the better part of the 18th century, the majority of the patrons using libraries were middle and upper class white people. Ethnic people did not use libraries but there is little or no evidence to show that this was because they were consciously kept out or whether librarians were uninformed as to how to serve them correctly. It wasn't until the turn of the 20th century that libraries started offering materials and services to different ethnic groups. Although some librarians realized that each ethnic group had its own culture, literature, music, etc. that was worth preserving, more emphasis was put on assimilating other cultures into the American way of life. Libraries provided services, story times, programs as well as materials in other languages as well as services to help immigrants in reading letters and other documents, sending messages to various governmental agencies, writing checks and filling out citizenship forms.

A bigger problem involving library services to ALL PEOPLE and one that was more far reaching than others was the fact that African Americans were being largely ignored as far as public libraries were concerned. In the South before the Civil War, African Americans were forbidden from reading. After the Civil War public libraries popped up around the South, but African Americans were not allowed to make use of these facilities, so, in reality, on this front little had changed. On into the 1930s the amount of funding for African American libraries did not accurately reflect the amount of people of that race in a given area. The services offered by these libraries, and many times they were few, were offered in segregated circumstances. African American branches were often poorly funded and were supported by the philanthropy of whites or churches of both races. Exceptions to the rule were the Louisville Free Public Library and its director, Thomas Fountion Blue, who took over in 1905; the Negro Branch Library in Nashville, Tennessee, which thrived under the leadership of Marian Hadley, who had trained under Thomas Blue, and Margaret Kercheval, who developed the children's collection and offered story hours.

In 1961 the American Library Association took a stand regarding service for African Americans and began insisting that library services for all people be equal. It probably won't be too much of a shock that not all communities were open to the idea of allowing African Americans to use their libraries. For example, the citizens of Danville and Petersburg, Virginia, voted to close their library rather than open it to black citizens.

As a lifelong southerner, and a proud one as well, I do have to say that problems of this type were not restricted to libraries below the Mason Dixon line. In *Foundations of Library and Information Science*, Richard E. Rubin states that there is evidence that northern libraries also engaged in discriminatory practices, but that this is generally over-looked. "For example, communities that received money from Andrew Carnegie's foundation often spent the money on the provision of service to whites in the community but not to African Americans; or far less money was spent resulting in inferior service. As the historian John Hope Franklin (1977) observed, 'one searches in vain for an indignant outcry on the part of the professional librarians against the profanation of their sacred profession and this subversion of their cherished institutions" (Rubin, p. 294).

The civil rights movement did see a change in library services for African Americans and other minorities, as legislation was put forth that would ensure that all would be welcome and would receive the same amount of service and level of satisfaction at their local library. The most important of these was the

Library Services and Construction Act which was passed in 1964. The LSCA provided funding for libraries to develop collections and services for different ethnic groups, the disadvantaged and other underserved groups—the homeless or the mentally ill, might be examples of this designation. Libraries have continued to evolve and services to groups that weren't always welcomed have improved. Is there still room for improvement in this aspect? Yes there is, there always will be need for improvement in this area and others, but I do have to say that libraries have done a far better job than a lot of other institutions in providing the best level of services to all people. Libraries are like living organisms that change and mature as time goes by. In the earliest civilization that produced the written work, libraries were there and have continued to be there and adapt to their environment, to change and morph themselves to provide the highest level of service to its patrons.

Before we put Library 101 behind us I do want to go into more detail about something that librarians will already know but something that will probably help the layman when reading a book covering all things library. Then again it may not help anything but it's good to know. That being all libraries are not born the same or created to fulfill the same role.

I mentioned that one of the first libraries in the U.S. was created when John Harvard donated 200 volumes to what would become the Harvard University Library. This library would at one time be the biggest library in America and is now the third largest library in the nation behind the Library of Congress and the Boston Public Library. The Harvard Library would be classified as an academic library, meaning that it serves a college or university. Librarians at academic libraries are charged with serving the students and faculty of their given institution, as well as making sense out of the Library of Congress classification system. I sort of started my library career when I was a student assistant at an academic library. As far as famous academic librarians or those academic librarians in pop culture, the sentient orangutan known only as the Librarian who oversees the massive library at Unseen University in Terry Pratchett's *Discworld* novels can be seen as an academic librarian.

To reiterate what was said a couple of paragraphs ago, the first true public library was the Boston Public Library or maybe the Peterborough, New Hampshire library. The duties of librarians at a public library, in addition to checking out books and other materials, is to serve as storytellers, technology experts, community programmers, reader's advisers, detectives and material reviewers and buyers. In a nutshell we rule. As for the list of fictional librarians that I have listed, Barbara "Batgirl" Gordon is a public librarian, eventually becoming the director of the Gotham Public Library. I don't think that they ever came right out and said it, but I would be willing to bet that Graveyard Gloria, from the *Porky's II* movie, was a public librarian. The library where she was picked up looked like a public library and she just has that vibe, you know what I'm saying? I guess I should apologize to all of the non-public librarians reading this, but you will find that this book is very public library centered. This is not meant as a slight. Every librarian and every library, no matter what type, has contributed to this profession greatly. The reason you will hear more public library stories than other types is because 95 percent of my professional experience has occurred in public libraries.

School librarians are sort of like academic librarians but they serve a school—elementary, middle, high, etc.—library. A lot of times these may be the first librarians that a child has any contact with. If the child was not taken to a public library by his or her parents, this will be his or her introduction. I remember when I was in school one of the things that always signaled the beginning of the school year was the tour of the library by the school librarian. She would show us where everything was, show us the procedure for checking out books, how to fill out the pocket cards, etc. It was a fond memory and these ladies and gentlemen have a very important job in introducing these children to the library and the wonders of reading. Buffy the Vampire Slayer's mentor Rupert Giles is a school librarian being the book jockey at Sunnydale High School where he can be present to point the slayer in the right direction.

Special libraries are just that, special. They are a great deal rarer and don't fit into the previously mentioned three categories. Special libraries are located in such places as businesses, newspapers, hospitals, private associations, the military and government agencies. There are also libraries that serve a particular population, such as the handicapped or a certain type of collection such as a presidential library. Flynn Carsen from *The Librarian* franchise and Evy from *The Mummy* movies both work in museum libraries, which would make them librarians in special libraries. There are also special librarians or information specialists who now work outside the typical library setting. They might work in one of the settings that I mentioned previously or in another situation. There are librarians known as information brokers, independent information professionals or information consultants. These can best be described as librarians for hire. When Barbara Gordon becomes the Oracle in DC Comics she is said to be an information broker.

Unknown Library Firsts

1. In 12,000 BC a cavewoman named Ne-Ne who was in charge of cataloging her tribe's extensive collection of tree bark tablets, pulled her hair back, stuck a fish bone through it and the first hair bun was born.

2. In 303 BC a man named Lom became the first problem patron when he walked into a Roman library and rolled some special herbs into one of the papyrus scrolls before lighting it on fire and attempting to smoke it.

3. A small donkey was the first overdue fine, collected from a young man when he returned a cuneiform tablet late to a Sumerian library in 2702 BC.

4. A Field Guide to Mammoths and Mastodons was the first non-fiction work to be checked out. The exact year and location has been lost to history.

5. Fifty Shades of Dirt was the first fiction work to be checked out. Specific date is unknown.

3

Let's Move the Library

I am of the belief that the good Lord puts certain people on this earth to do certain things. You can judge this by one, talent (how else could Mozart compose a symphony at age 3?) and two, just the situations that put them on the path to that exact destination. I believe I'm the latter because within a couple of months of graduating college, for the first time, I interviewed for a job at my hometown library. Did I get the job? Well, no, but just a few days after receiving the dreaded denial letter in the mail I was contacted by the director telling me that the head of reference would be out of work to have surgery for six weeks and would I accept a temporary position to help cover the reference desk during his absence. Of course I accepted and my first post-college library job was working the reference desk at the public library, a full forty hours a week.

It was during this time that, for the first time, I encountered a creature that has put many a librarian on their heels, that being the difficult patron, scientific name *Bitchiest Witchianus*. I was at the reference desk, of course, and a woman came in looking for a book by Hal Lindsey. Hal Lindsey is one of those apocalyptic authors who predicts the end of the world every few years or so. This woman said that her sister had checked out the book, that it was wonderful and that she had to have it. I checked the card catalog (this was before computers so it was the wood and brass variety with the drawers full of little cards.) I couldn't find it so I asked the lady to wait, which she didn't like, and checked the locater. The locater was about the size and weight of a Buick and was shaped like a really big desk. You would hit a button with the range of letters that the author's name fell between and a chain drive would pull around the appropriate drawer and the cards corresponding to that author and that title. This is how we could tell if there were any other copies of a particular title at the other county libraries. There weren't.

We had the only copy and it was out, so I had to go tell Aunt Bea that the book was checked out.

"That can't be! My sister had it, you're wrong!"

"No ma'am, the book is checked out. Did your sister turn it back in?"

"Yes she certainly did! You don't know what you're talking about! I'll just go find somebody who knows their way around this place!"

"Thank you, come again." Then I went back to the reference desk and the charm school queen stomped up toward the lending desk. In a few minutes one of the ladies working lending came back to where I was and gave her assessment of the lady's character.

"That woman you just dealt with was a grouchy old biddy wasn't she?" I just nodded, not thinking that I had been working there long enough to call a patron a "grouchy old biddy." Apparently the woman had given lending a hard time as well. Then she went out into the lobby, used the pay phone—it was the days when they were still around—and called her sister, who still had the book, like I said she had.

I learned a lot during the six weeks that I was a temporary employee at the Library. Before long it was over, the head of reference was back and I was unemployed again. I had liked the library. I had liked the people and got the feeling that the fondness was reciprocated. I also knew this was what I wanted to do as a career. I went home and started combing the want ads again, looking for jobs in libraries as well as jobs that would tide me over until I found a library job. Positions of that type that I had applied for and, thankfully did not get, included, among others, selling perfume and selling pool tables. I will truthfully tell anyone that I am a horrible salesman, so it's good that I did not get a position selling anything! Then in a little over a week I got a call from the head of reference, the man whom I had replaced when I was a temporary employee. He informed me that the page, a part-time job usually reserved for high school students and retirees, involving shelving and other more basic duties, had quit and would I like the job. So I had the opportunity to go back to the library that I had honestly enjoyed, and work as long as I wanted, and didn't piss anybody off that bad. My answer—remember I haven't always been the sharpest of tools—was, "No thanks, I'm looking for something full time." Yes, I was that dumb and I planned on sticking to that, until I told my fiancée and she showed why she is and always will be the smartest of the pair.

"It's getting your foot in the door, call him back. It's a job." I sort of made this mumbly protest which I guess meant, "I don't want to!" If you really want to read this statement in the way that it was meant to be, picture me with my bottom lip out T-Rex arms flailing, stomping the floor like a three-year-old. As is often the

3. Let's Move the Library

Me doing a karate demonstration at the branch library.

case, she won and, in a rare moment of clarity (or was it intimidation) I agreed to accept the job until I found something else, a permanent library position. The next morning I slumped into the library and walked up to the reference desk. The head of reference, I'll call him Mr. Duncan, was standing behind the desk with the other reference librarian. They looked to be deep in a non-library related conversation and they looked at me like they had expected me to come in at any time. I very penitently walked up to the desk and told Mr. Duncan that I had reconsidered and would like to take the job after all. I hoped that he hadn't filled the position yet and that he wouldn't laugh me out of the place. He simply said: "Oh, well okay come on back." And I was then a permanent employee of the main branch of our Public Library. It would take me close to twenty years before I found "something else."

Libraries in our county date back to 1819, according to legislative records. It wasn't until 1936, however, that a group of young women began a campaign for a town library in the county seat. During an episode of *The Andy Griffith Show*,

Andy tells cheap Barney Fife knockoff Warren that there are three rules to a happy life in Mayberry: (1) Don't play leapfrog with elephants; (2) Don't pet a tiger unless his tail is wagging; and (3) Never, ever, mess with the Ladies' Auxiliary. I would add to that, never mess with any gaggle of women, large or small, because they tend to get things done, for good or for evil. This small group of women met at a house to play bridge when the conversation kept coming back to the town's need for a public library. They started a club for the specific purpose of starting a library. This club became an association and was incorporated in 1951 and still exists at this very moment. They started with no money, no books, no appropriate location and no librarians to staff the place. They set about holding countless fundraisers of every type and before long had funds, books and two rooms above a drug store rent free. The library opened for business in February 1936 and, despite a large snowfall, checked out 384 books the first day. The library operated in that location until the following year when it moved to the basement of the armory. Then in 1939 it moved to a room at city hall that had been designated specifically for the library. In 1940 the commissioners founded the county library system after state aid became available for those counties, 52 in all, who applied for it. There were already three municipal libraries at that time, including the facility that the ladies founded four years earlier. State aid amounted to $900 that first year and county appropriation was $50 a month. The library stayed at the armory building until 1964 when the city opened a building to be designated as the library. It was there that a certain bright-eyed and bushy tailed young librarian cut his teeth in the library world. On April 6, 1993, voters approved a referendum for an addition to the building. We will discuss this matter in depth a little later.

Just a word about Duncan. He was sort of a polarizing figure around the library. A lot of our fellow staff members didn't seem to like him and I guess I could see why. He could be cantankerous and he was definitely not a people person. I have seen few people better on the administrative side of the running of the library, the paperwork and the knowledge of the collection. His talents for dealing with the public, however, were a stark contrast to his talent behind the desk. This would soon lead him to accept a job elsewhere and, to be quite honest, I missed him. Despite some of the other librarians' opinions concerning him, I liked him. He was one of the sort of delightfully weird, quirky people that I gravitate to. Other than that, he was a movie buff which was something we had in common and his knowledge of the subject was pretty vast. What I liked about Mr. Duncan the most was his cranky sense of humor. Let me illustrate. One morning we were unpacking a large box of paperbacks that somebody had donated to the library. As it turns out the great majority of them were paperback romances and Duncan wasted no time in expressing his scorn for this particular art form.

One of the books had a rather lurid cover with a Fabio look alike embracing a raven haired beauty with her bosoms hiked up under her chin by a medieval style bodice. The tagline across the bottom of the cover read: "Breathtaking Adventure and Searing Romance!" Mr. Duncan mockingly read the title as well as this tagline and then tossed the book into the box with the rest of the others.

"Breathtaking adventure and searing romance," he snorted, "If I wanted any of that I would go find some." It should be said that Mr. Duncan was not married, never married, lived alone and, as far as I know, never went on a single date. I don't know where he had planned on going to find his "breathtaking adventure" or his "searing romance" and he never elaborated. He did have an eye for the ladies, however. Once after waiting on an EXTREMELY HOT blue-eyed blonde, he turned to me with an indignant look on his face and as he talked he poked the top of the reference desk with his finger like he was arguing a point in court. "It ought to be a law for any one person to look that good!"

One of Mr. Duncan's quirks involved his devotion to the Wake Forest Demon Deacons, which was not his alma mater. Regardless, I think he had previously volunteered at the campus radio station and was blindly devoted to the sports teams. During football and basketball season he would wear the same gold tie with the same black shirt on game days. At the beginning of football season he would run out of the reference office and raise a finger to the ceiling like he was signaling for the kick off. Then he would trot a couple of steps and kick one foot up high like he was sending the pigskin eighty yards down the field. At the beginning of basketball season he would come out of the office with just as much zeal, dribble one hand and turn a couple of times like he was evading defenders and then he would do a very clumsy jump shot to make the winning pretend basket.

This library was where I felt I was meant to be and it did feel like things had just fallen in line to put me there. My duties as page were a little different than my predecessor. Since I was a college graduate with experience in the library field, rather than a high school student, they included the normal, shelving books (my favorite activity), shelf reading, and checking in the mail, but they also included a great deal of time at the reference desk although it was down from forty hours, but still more than if the job had been filled by a teenager.

I also did much the same thing in the Extension Department. The Extension Department is what, at our library, the bookmobile evolved into. I would venture a guess that the great majority of people reading these words have heard, seen or used the bookmobile. If not, let me describe it to you. It's a mobile library that allows library staff to get out into the community, to the schools and to people who maybe wouldn't get to the library otherwise. The present bookmobile at the library system I work for is a large R.V. sized vehicle complete with shelves that allow patrons to enter and browse just like they would do in an actual library. I have also seen bookmobiles that reminded me of the catering trucks that frequented factories and mills, that is when they were still open for operation. These bookmobiles were smaller, maybe pick-up truck sized and had panels in the rear where a camper would be on a truck and they would fold up to expose shelves filled with books. There were even some that were pulled by horses and were situated on the backs of horses in the days before trucks became readily available.

In 1938 our library, with the cooperation of the State Library Commission and the Works Progress Administration, or the W.P.A., and the county commissioners had a bookmobile brought to the county for a month. This was to show the citizenry how cheap and convenient such a vehicle would be. This demonstration model, filled with books, made its rounds to the counties of the state of North Carolina to demonstrate the worth of such a vehicle. In 1943 the county received a full time bookmobile from the State Library Commission, a Ford truck which was previously used by the W.P.A. It came stocked with books that were donations to the Commission when the W.P.A. ceased operation. With gas being in short supply during World War II this bookmobile served a valuable service bringing material to the citizens of the county. Another bookmobile, a Chevy van with shelves on both sides, was purchased in 1948. A walk in variety like the one that I previously mentioned was bought in 1956 and stayed in use until 1972. After that it was decided that school libraries had improved as well as the municipal libraries so the bookmobile wasn't replaced. Instead the Extension Department was created to serve the same purpose.

When I was there the library had a couple of Ford minivans and two staff members who would take them out, along with several large canvas bags, to make deliveries to several daycares and shut-ins throughout the county. On paper this looks like it was a pretty easy going job, but I can tell you it was a lot more involved than it seems, although I never went out on deliveries myself. On top of delivering books to daycares, the Extension Department did story times and other programs. Their other service involved going to people's houses who were designated shut-ins and had signed up for this service. These were people who were invalid or for some other reason could not come out to the library, so the Extension Department would deliver books and other materials for them. These materials had been requested by the patrons and checked out before the item ever left the library. Once they were delivered, the materials that they already had checked out had to be retrieved, taken back to the library and checked in. From what I understand sometimes this involved rooting through somebody's house in an attempt to find a book or books that had simply been laid down and forgotten.

It was around this time that I was introduced to a library phenomenon that has since interested me a great deal, the Strange Patron, also known as *Batshittidae Crazius*. I don't know how it is in other types of libraries, (I haven't worked in anything other than public libraries since college) but in a public library setting you will have around a half dozen, sometimes more, patrons who are completely off their rocker. This may range from mildly eccentric to stone cold crazy, but they always number about six and when one crazy patron leaves another will be there to take his or her place. It could be a law, I don't know for sure, but that's how it is and has been since I've been working in libraries, probably since the days of the Sumerian libraries, and it will probably be like this for as long as they exist.

When I had still been a temp I was told about the King and Queen who had been regular patrons for years and would come in at least daily, sometimes multiple times a day. Despite their regal titles they were a rather disheveled pair and no one was really sure of their relation to one another, husband/wife, boyfriend/girlfriend, brother/sister, maybe two or more relationships fit their situation. No one was sure and no one seemed willing to ask. The queen always wore a wig that was a dramatically different color than her real hair and was too small for her head so it sort of sat on top of her dome like a hat, or should I say, crown. The queen's favorite pastimes in the library were to berate the staff and photocopy her jewelry. She labored under the delusion that some nefarious person or persons had plotted to steal the plastic jewelry that she always wore, so she made it a point to photocopy it quite often just in case, severely scarring the copier's glass in the process.

The king mostly just loped along behind the queen and played the quiet one in the relationship. One time, however, he was involved in one very comical, very loud altercation with another rather colorful patron. The patron in question was an elderly retired doctor who lived a couple of doors down from the library and who would come in daily and monopolize the *Wall Street Journal* for the better part of the morning. He was hard of hearing so he talked with the volume of a jet taking off and had constant often resonant flatulence, which must have made a quiet morning in the library extremely pleasant. Apparently one day the king decided that the doctor had read the paper long enough and tried to take it from him. The ensuing fight was loud and was made even more exciting by the intervention of Duncan who was an excitable character himself. Between all the yelling, the farting and the raining of newsprint down onto the table nearby, it was especially entertaining to those people who didn't have to deal with it.

As I have said, I've always felt that I was directed into the library profession, sort of like I was dropped on a slippery sliding board and the library was at the bottom. There was nothing I could have done, even if I had wanted to, to keep me out of the library. Library school, however, wouldn't be quite as straight forward. To become a professional librarian and to rise within the ranks of the profession without hindrance requires a masters in library science, or masters in library and information studies, depending on when and where you got your degree. I knew that, I had learned that in college, but I hadn't taken it to heart quickly enough to repair the damage to my grades that my life as a slacker musician had done to it. There's a top notch library school at a state university just up the road from where I live. It is a well-thought-of program and a great majority of the people whom I've worked with received their degrees at this particular institution. All I had to do was get in. That was the problem. My grades in college were not good enough to get me in on their own. My first attempt at taking the Graduate Record Exam didn't help. First off, for someone with my attention span, sitting in a desk in a classroom for three hours filling in countless little circles with a pencil was nothing short of hell and my scores showed that. In a nutshell I had a job, admittedly a part-time one, and I was getting experience. The next problem was to get my degree. I just couldn't get accepted into the program.

At that same time I was taking a couple of library science classes at the university as a special student, which meant that I was allowed to take the classes but I was not a full-time student. These classes did not count toward a degree and I didn't get a faculty adviser to sort of steer me along like the legitimate students. I still had questions, however, so one night after class I went by the library science department to see if any of the professors were there and would be willing to help me out. There was one professor there so I knocked on his door and asked if I could run a few questions by him. He consented and I left three hours later feeling a lot better about things. This particular professor has to be one of my favorite teachers I have had in any degree and I would definitely consider him a mentor. He's a colorful character with a penchant for wearing flowered vests and bowties. I'll call him Dr. Beauregard because he's from the Deep South and I could always see him sitting on the front porch of an antebellum style mansion drinking mint juleps. Not only did he answer my questions about libraries and graduate school, but he also instilled in me the knowledge and the confidence of what it took to succeed. He confided in me that he did not get into the Ph.D. program at UNC–Chapel Hill the first time he tried.

"I'm not very bright," he told me. "But I'm awfully persistent." That's something that I've not only remembered, but taken to heart.

The agreement with my future alma mater was that I was to take the classes as a special student and make at least a B, preferably an A, for the university to consider admitting me. I did not live up to my end of the bargain. Remembering what my favorite professor told me, I kept my nose to the grindstone and signed up for two more classes outside the library science department, a history class on managing archives and an archaeology class. The first class was pretty uneventful; the second, while a really fun class, I dropped because of poor performance. The teacher looked a lot like Janis Joplin and wore flannel shirts, jeans and work boots to class. She was a neat lady, very funny. A couple of my favorite things that she said were that Crista galli sounded like a stripper and that the humerus wasn't that funny.

> Crista galli (crista gal-e) n. An upright process on the anterior portion of the cribriform plate to which the anterior form of the falx cerebri is attached. *Merriam Webster Online Dictionary.*
>
> Cribriform Plate (kr-b'rY-fôrm ' pleit) n. The horizontal plate of the ethmoid bone perforated with numerous foramina for the passage of the olfactory nerve filaments from the nasal cavity called also lamina cribrosa. *Merriam Webster Online Dictionary.*
>
> Ethmoid Bone (Eth ' moid ' bohn) n. a light spongy cubical bone of the.... Oh forget it. The Crista galli is in your skull! And the humerus is in your arm!

I enjoyed talking to her, but dropped the class when I figured that I wouldn't make the required B. Needless to say this did not get me into library school so, once again, I dropped back and punted.

Shortly after I starting working at my hometown library on a permanent basis, plans were put in motion to renovate the old building. You remember I mentioned that in 1993 a bond referendum had been voted through to renovate the library. Long before I got there the library had run out of space, which is a problem that every library has, remember the Sumerian libraries. In every library I have ever been in there has never been enough space, the roof leaks and the climate control never works to suit every member of the staff.

The plan was to move everything out of the library building and move it to a temporary location while the old building was renovated. If this sounds like a daunting task, you have no idea, and it just so happened that I was just settled into my first permanent library position just in time for the first trial of Hercules.

The first time that my then fiancée came to the library was when we were breaking the library down and hauling everything out. That morning Mr. Duncan had taken one of the library's doors off the hinges, laid it flat, drilled holes through it, and mounted plastic castors into it. His plan was to use the door as a dolly to take load after load of old, outdated magazines which had been molding in the storage room, out to be discarded in a dumpster which had been transported to the library parking lot. Just as my future wife and I had entered the building,

Duncan, after piling a metric ton of magazines on this makeshift dolly, tried to direct it down a thin aisle between the shelves near the loading dock. It was there that the plastic wheels buckled under the weight, hemming the dolly and its shipment between the shelves. By the time we had said our hellos to the rest of the staff and walked into the storage area, Duncan was in the middle of a full blown meltdown. When we got there he had been trying to climb over and around the dolly and had slid down onto his butt on the floor, between the broken platform, the magazines and the shelf. Then he struggled to his feet, threw a Sharpie across the room and began kicking random objects and cursing. I have heard a lot of profanity, and used a lot in my day, but never so much strung together like that, it was enough to make your ears burn and while I have to admit that I was somewhat impressed by Duncan's verbal clinic, my fiancée was not. When he had calmed down to a point that I dared approach him, I introduced him to my future wife. He immediately stopped, smiled politely and gave a very courtly bow. I don't think that did a lot to improve her opinion of him, but he was nice nevertheless, at least for a minute.

The plan that administration had written out for the move called for all the books in the library collection to be packed in boxes which were numbered in sequence and then the National Guard would pack them in the back of one of their trucks, in sequence, would ship them, in sequence to the temporary location, which was an old grocery store across town and unload them, in sequence. During the packing process we found that the best free boxes to be found were liquor boxes which could be found by the truckload at the local liquor store. Even when you take the logical reason for using them into account I must say that it was still humorous to see a library full of dozens of Everclear, Jack Daniels and Smirnoff boxes.

> Speaking of Everclear I have a great story concerning that particular libation. It doesn't relate to libraries, or anything else in this book for that matter, but it's too funny not to tell. When we were in college we had a hall mate who was a big drinker, even bigger than the rest of us. One night this friend of ours planned a little party for us in he and his roommate's room. For the party he purchased a fifth of Everclear and some Welch's grape juice to mix it with, a case and a half of beer and, for himself, a fresh, unopened pack of cigarettes and a hamburger from a local greasy spoon. Well, this friend of ours started hitting the Everclear and Welch's a little early and was passed out on his bunk by 9 o'clock as the party kept going on around him. Sometime during the evening his roommate's girlfriend, who had a talent for applying make-up, did the sleeping man's face. She did his eyes, applied lipstick, brought out his cheek-

3. Let's Move the Library

bones and blended it expertly. I have to say that he was almost attractive in a Monty Python type of way.

The next morning I had just woken up and was lying there trying to talk myself into getting out of bed when I heard the heavy drinker in his room across the hall.

"What the Hell!" I got up and went straight to his room. He was standing in the middle of what can justifiably be called a disaster area. He was surrounded by empty beer cans and was holding a ball of cellophane in one hand and his hamburger in the other. "When I went to bed," he barked, "I had part of a fifth of Everclear, a case and a half of beer, a pack of cigarettes and a hamburger! There's the Everclear!" He gestured to the clear, bone dry bottle that had been slung into the corner. "You can see what happened to the beer!" He waved a hand around him to the crumpled beer cans. "Here's what's left of the cigarettes." (The wadded up piece of cellophane.) "and here's the hamburger." The burger had a huge bite taken out of it. I will admit to being a part of this crime wave but I will not take responsibility for all of it. Also remember that during this little rant of his, his face was still covered in women's make-up except that by now it had all smeared so he sort of looked like a cheap hooker after a long night.

The day when the collection was finally loaded up and sent to the temporary location was on a Friday. It was to be shipped and unloaded, in sequence, there. When we got there the boxes had been delivered but rather than being unloaded in sequence, the National Guard had unloaded the boxes and piled them in the middle of the floor, not in sequence. There was a lot of the tearing of clothes and gnashing of teeth, not to mention cursing. I will never forget the sight of all those pissed off librarians glaring up at a pile of books that was almost stacked to the ceiling and Mr. Duncan teetering on top of it trying to find some way to spread these boxes out and get them into the proper order. Remember it was Duncan that I replaced when he was out for surgery? Well it was surgery on his inner ear which greatly affected his balance, so it wasn't like he was standing tall on top of the stack like King Kong on top of the Empire State Building, he was weaving and wobbling, a yellow construction worker's hat balanced precariously on top of his head, and several of the staff members were running around under him to catch him in anticipation of his fall.

It should be said that according to the *Whole Library Handbook*, Persian vizier Abdul Kassem Ismae traveled with 400 camels that bore his library which numbered into hundred of thousands of volumes. The camels were trained to walk in an order that ensured that the books stayed in sequence. Maybe we should have used camels instead of soldiers.

The books were eventually sorted. Furniture, supplies and huge heavy ranges of shelving were carried in by the staff. The 18-ton locator was, thankfully moved by maintenance. I think that everybody had at least one meltdown during this period. I remember I was putting some carefully sequenced books on a shelf which was missing a peg under one of the front corners causing the shelf to tip forward and dump the books out onto the floor.

"What the @#$! is wrong with this #$#@! shelf!" I yelled. "It keeps dumping the $#$#@ books onto the &*$#@ floor! What the $$@#!" A co-worker of mine simply walked over and, without a word, replaced the peg, sat the shelf right and replaced the books. Then she walked off and went back to what she was doing. I was left feeling a little bit like I was wearing blue jeans in a tuxedo world.

While we were in the temporary facility we dealt with burned out ballasts in the light fixtures, which would drip tar and smelled like burning tires. We also shared a wall with a batting cage so on occasion a foul ball would smack the opposite wall and roust all the sleeping readers out of their slumber. One time we were having trouble with flooding in the back room and when maintenance looked into the problem they pulled a dead cat out of the drain with a Roto-Rooter. Now on the whole librarians are animal people, a lot are cat people, so to some of the staff this was very disturbing. To others of us it was mildly humorous, in a dark, Tim Burton sort of way.

The thing about the layout of the library, remember this was an old grocery store, is that the different departments shared the same ceiling with the shelves being the only walls, so whatever happened in one department could be heard throughout the library, the reference office, the genealogy room and the children's room. Lending and reference were right beside each other and, again, shared the uniform ceiling. The head of the lending department was a dear sweet woman who would become like another mother over the years. I nicknamed her Queenie because of her tendency to act rather high falootin'. Queenie had the idea that everybody, and I mean everybody, should aggressively seek out a significant other so that they could get married and have children. If she felt that a co-worker was not pursuing this end ardently enough, then she would "help" them. One day one of the reference librarians was assisting a very attractive young lady and Queenie was intently watching the transaction. When it ended Queenie watched with some disappointment as the woman left and the co-worker made no move to further the relationship.

"He needs to get on top of her real quick!" Queenie said and her words were broadcast all over the library. It was only after she had already said them that she realized what she had said and collapsed into her trademark, high-pitched cackle.

I got married right before the library moved back to its permanent location.

3. Let's Move the Library

I got married on a Saturday and if memory serves me correctly, Thursday was my last day before the nuptials. That morning a "honeymoon survival kit" mysteriously showed up on my desk. Included in this kit was a container of hangover helper, some aspirin, sore muscle ointment, a jar of Vaseline and a box of condoms that were of too large a size to be used effectively. I have never been able to find out who left the kit, I always suspected that Queenie was involved, but nobody ever fessed up to it. I've been told over the years that if someone were to do that these days that it would surely result in some sort of lawsuit. I personally have never been that litigious. Second, it was funny and I have laughed about it off and on over the years. The fact that a borderline offensive joke could be pulled off at work with no lawsuits and with nothing but mirth and good feelings as a result should be an indicator of how close the staff at that library was. The librarians that went through that move were the same, give or take, that would man that library for the next ten or fifteen years. We did get close. We went through a lot together and a great many practical jokes were shared over the years.

Things to Remember When Moving Your Library

1. Liquor stores and grocery stores provide the best free boxes. Remember that books, in numbers, are heavy. The architect who designed my hometown library's renovation told me that libraries and paper companies have to hold more pounds per square inch than most other buildings. Therefore the boxes that you move the books in should be sturdy and both of these types are, especially the liquor boxes which are accustomed to holding several bottles of hooch at a time. In addition you don't run the risk of them smelling like onions or ripe bananas and transferring that smell to the books. I found a large onion in one box from a grocery store and hid it in one of the drawers of Queenie's desk, taking care to rub it on everything first. I was chastised for that and had said onion tossed at me in retaliation.

2. Moving a library is stressful so have some sort of counselor on site, either that or a wet bar. Take it from me you won't find stray liquor bottles in the boxes. The clerks at the liquor stores check them really thoroughly.

3. A patron once suggested that we should have a candy machine in the library that distributed Xanax. Such a device would definitely come in handy in this situation.

4. Don't have the National Guard move anything that needs to stay in sequence, use camels.

5. If you're moving into an old building, check the pipes for dead pets.

6. Be very nice to the maintenance department. Bribery couldn't hurt either.

4

Library School, Finally!

After getting married and helping to move the library to and from the temporary facility, I once again started directing my efforts towards getting into the library science program. I had taken classes, both in and out of the department, as a special student and tanked, so this time I actually enrolled in the English Department at that same institution to get a second bachelors and hopefully prove myself academically and ensure the M.L.S. Department that I had matured since I had graduated from college the first time.

While I was applying to the English Department and waiting for their response I sought some counsel from a great many people, librarians yes, but also counselors, psychiatrists and neurologists. Since I can remember I have had a little too much energy, was a little too excitable and had a hard time paying attention to pretty much anything that didn't involve monsters and space ships. When I was little what a heard most was that "I was not living up to my potential," "What is wrong with you?" and a couple of times I was called "lazy." Although these symptoms have lessened a little since I have gotten older, they've never really gone away. Throughout my life I have been told that I have attention deficit disorder, hyperactivity, depression, stress-related anxiety and bi polar disorder. Did I ever believe these diagnoses? Maybe so and maybe not. As I started trying to achieve my second bachelors I was diagnosed with adult ADD and given a prescription of Ritalin which I only took a couple of doses of. Did the Ritalin focus my attention? Sure, for a couple of hours it did just that. The crash, however, was like going from 100 miles an hour to a stand still in .1000 of a second. During this time I was described as "down" and "angry." After the second or third dose I flushed the rest and had a little talk with the man in the mirror. Did it work? Well I graduated with a B.A. in English and a 3.4

GPA, up from 2.0 the first time I graduated college. So, I would have to say yes.

I also retook the G.R.E., Graduate Record Exam, and was able to go about it in a different way that better served my purposes and my particular personality. The way that I took it first was to sit in a classroom for three and a half hours and fill out little bubbles with a pencil. I think this is a level of punishment reserved for the ninth level of Hell. The next time I took the G.R.E. I was able to sit in a classroom and take it by computer. The reason this is different, and a million times better, is that you could take it at your own pace. If you wanted to use the restroom, get something to drink or just stretch your legs you could do so because you were being watched through a closed circuit TV as well as through a two way mirror. This really made a difference and my scores were a great deal better than the first time.

After I had gotten a B.A. in English and after I had taken the G.R.E. again I called the professor who oversaw admissions for the M.L.S. Department. I had called her office many times over the previous five years. By this time she had long learned my voice.

"Okay, okay," she said, sounding very harried and frustrated. "You're in, you're in."

So in the fall semester of 1999, after around a half decade of trying, I officially enrolled in the library science department at this local institution. One of the first people I met after I started working toward my masters was Dr. Beauregard who had been so nice to advise me that night when I was a special student.

"We have heard some great things about you," he said, which let me start the program on a positive note and a firm belief in myself that I could succeed in the program.

Until the mid–19th century there was no formal training for librarians. You were on your own to develop your skills and follow the examples of others. Sometimes a young librarian might seek out the counsel of a more established librarian, but it wasn't until between 1850 and 1875 that a formal system of apprenticeship was put in place. During this procedure a budding librarian would work under another more experienced one under the latter's close supervision. Another route to professional development was through professional magazines. *Publishers Weekly* was, as the name implies, devoted to the publishing industry but included a small section for librarians and library related information. The *American Library Journal*, which was eventually renamed *Library Journal* was first published in 1876 and would prove to be the main publication for the profession and the first one to be devoted specifically to the library field. *Library Journal* published articles, summaries of A.L.A. conference proceedings and a section called "Notes and Queries" which were the answers to questions from librarians that were sent in to them.

In the late 1800s there was a boom of libraries in this country which, in turn called for more library workers, including trained librarians. As this period wore on, the training of librarians went from a more scholarly bent, from journals and associations, to a more formal process of instruction; still the education of librarians stubbornly stayed within the old method of apprenticeship until 1883 when Melville Dewey began talks with Columbia College, now University, in New York City, to not only apply as head librarian, but start a formal program to professionally train librarians. Early in 1887 the School of Library Economy opened with a total enrollment of 20, 3 men and 17 women. The fact that Dewey had insisted on enrolling women was a point of contention between he and Columbia's board of trustees, and this tension would eventually lead to the closing of that program. You would like to think that Dewey insisted on women being enrolled in this program to be trained in a profession that they would form the great majority of, out of a wish for equal opportunity for women, but there are some who believe that he simply wanted a place to keep his hands. If I'm being too subtle let me elaborate. There are rumors that when he was around women he took a fancy to, Melville turned into the proverbial octopus. He grew three more pairs of hands which would fly everywhere, pinching, squeezing and groping. So we can't really hold him up as the icon of equal opportunity, more like a Hugh Hefner with a beard.

The curriculum of early library schools included such practical subjects as reader's aids, bibliography, the repair of library materials, and administration. Another subject offered by many of these programs is what would come to be called "library hand." It was a standardized form of writing developed by Dewey and Thomas Edison to ensure that library materials' labels, registers and the like would always be inscribed in a legible manner. Instruction in library hand was widespread until typewriters were widely available.

By the time that I came along typewriters were not only widely available but technology had gotten to the point that they were on the way out. Technology was becoming the backbone of libraries and the library profession.

Here's a list of the classes I took while I was enrolled in library school.

LIS 600 or Foundations of Library and Information Studies. One note. I do not know if these classes still have the same class numbers or names, I'm using the ones that were designated when I attended. LIS 600 is the class that most start with and is a historical survey of libraries, their operations and potential roles in society. It basically gives you an introduction to the program and to library science in general. It was unusual starting the program and being in this class having over five years of experience in an actual library. There was a mixture in class of idealistic bright eyed students and somewhat jaded people who had already gotten their feet wet and knew why people could not be allowed to look at pornography in the library and couldn't be given willy nilly to do anything they wanted to. The mix made for a great class and presented many different views of the issues we discussed.

LIS 620, Information Sources and Services, or reference as we call it. I was looking forward to this class because, most of my experience has been in the reference department and the Dr. Beauregard who had given me so much encouragement was the professor. The course was very interesting and entertaining but involved a lot of work. One of the assignments involved answering a series of questions. A question in this assignment might read as follows: "There is a wine that is manufactured in a region of France through which runs a river named after a goddess who was worshiped in a particular Greek city state. There was a battle in this region where a legendary warrior distinguished himself. Who was that warrior? What was his weapon of choice and what was his grandmother's roommate's cousin's name?" The thing is, if you don't get the first fact right you want get any of them, so it's important to get each and every fact correct.

There is also another assignment called a pathfinder which is basically a report based on a specific subject, but the project is more on the resources—print, visual, electronic, etc.—that you would use to research this topic. My pathfinder was on sports humor, yes the topics are chosen by the student, and my project was a very involved study on the methods and materials you would use to form a study of sports humor, from the subject headings that would help you to locate these subjects to the materials themselves.

LIS 613, Business Sources and Services, was a more specific class concerning, as the title illustrates, the proper use of sources that center on businesses and business practices. Our main project was to take a business, research it and follow it on the stock market throughout the semester. I chose Pixar who, at the time was mostly known for the movie, *Toy Story* but has since released countless animated features. It was interesting to find information on the company, but the fact that, due to a deal with Disney where that company kept the majority of the profits, Pixar's cost per share never rose or fell throughout the semester, which made this company a rather boring subject.

LIS 640, Organizing Library Collections, or cataloging was not a fun class and my only "B." Cataloging is the technique involved in processing materials into the system so they can be checked in and out. It is detail work so, as you can guess, not up my alley. It's sort of the polar opposite to reference, a lot of librarians like one or the other, not both. In my opinion if the G.R.E. is the ninth layer of Hell, then studying cataloging must be somewhere along the 3rd or 4th.

LIS 650, Library Administration and Management, was a great class of which I was privileged to be involved in. The one question that I have for those people involved in administration and management is that, seeing how squirrely people are—and I'm not talking about a specific person or group just people in general—can you prepare for management by taking a class? Is there anything that can prepare you for management? Is it sort of like classes in parenting?

LIS 611, Humanities Information Sources, was a class a lot like Business Sources and Services just placing emphasis on the fields of philosophy, literature, theater, cinema and TV, music art, religion folklore and mythology. It was taught by my favorite professor, Dr. Beauregard from reference class, so we had pathfinders to do. I did mine on Gothic literature and embarrassed myself slightly in class when I meant to say the title of the Flannery O'Connor short story, *A Good Man Is Hard to Find*. Instead I said, "A hard man is good to find." The funny part is that somebody in the class, without skipping a beat said: "Oh how true." Another part that I remember from this class is, after the first session we changed rooms. I don't know if he was serious but Dr. Beauregard said that it was because the color of the walls made him want to jump out of a window.

LIS 688, Intellectual Freedom Seminar, examined issues of intellectual freedom in libraries. Most people limit this to censorship and it was included in the seminar, just not limited to it. It also included access to print governmental information, current and future access to technology, copyrights and privacy concerns. The censorship angle had always been a favorite topic of mine and one that many people profess to be against, that is until somebody says something that they don't like. You really get to see how open minded you are when somebody skewers your own sacred white buffalo. I remember the first class the professor had the class give yourself a rating from one to ten regarding your beliefs on intellectual freedom. One means that you're a complete fascist and you don't believe that people should have access to any information. Ten means that you believe people should have access to anything at any time. I gave myself a five because I had long established my aforementioned belief that people will rant and rave against censorship until it is them who are being offended. There was another guy in the class who gave himself a 10, that is he was wide open to people's access to entertainment and information. A couple of sessions later we were talking about works that parody others. At this time the book, *The Wind Done Gone* had just been released which is a parody of *Gone with the Wind*. The estate of Margaret Mitchell, the author of *Gone with the Wind*, had attempted to block the release of the novel. Thing is, parody is protected speech and not subject to restriction by copyright. The teacher was asking if this is an ethical practice or should it be changed. I made the statement that, as a budding author myself, not only would I not care if someone parodied one of my works but I would see it as a chance for interest in the original works to be generated with little work on my part. I had hardly gotten these words out of my mouth when Mr. 10 made the statement: "Well nobody likes to be made fun of." To this the professor reminded him of his self declared rank.

Another session that I liked in this particular class was when the professor had the local legislator who was the head of the congressional committee that regulated copyrights and patents, which is another subject included in intellectual freedom discussions. What I liked about the class was that the legislator and the professor, who were on completely different ends of the political spectrum, led a very orderly and respectful discussion on this topic and stayed away from partisan politics.

LIS 615, Collection Management, or study of the procedures involved in building a library collection involving development, evaluation and maintenance. A funny occurrence in this class happened when we were discussing the two different classification systems, Library of Congress vs. the Dewey Decimal System. The teacher who was wearing a cardigan sweater buttoned to the neck, typical librarian garb, stood up and ripped it open like Superman to reveal a Dewey Decimal System "Numbers you can count on!" t-shirt.

LIS 655, The Public Library, covers the librarian as an administrator and financial and cooperative planner, as well as library services and community analysis.

LIS 605a, Website Design and Management, covers the design and management of Internet sites. We designed websites by typing the individual codes, no HTML editors were allowed. I designed a website that promoted my writing and included several of my short stories on the site with its own site decorated to correspond with the theme of the short story. For example, I included a story that occurs on Halloween. It was decorated with Halloween colors and "monster-type" decorations, flying bats, spiders, large malevolent eyes, etc.

LIS 688A, Library Services for Adults, One of the main grades for this class was for the class to split up and work as a team to develop a study of a topic that dealt with services for adults. Our group's project centered on senior adults and library technology. I wanted to call the study, "That's a Mouse Not a Pedal," but I was shot down. I was actually the person who suggested this particular topic. I've always thought that libraries put a lot of attention toward appealing to children and teens, which is an important endeavor, but older people shouldn't be forgotten. At the time I was teaching computer classes at my hometown library and seniors made up a good amount of my students. They enjoy the library, they'll support the library but they have serious concerns about technology and how to use it, so that was what made me suggest that particular topic and the rest of the group ran with it.

> The reference to "that's a mouse not a pedal" came from one of my favorite "people learning to use technology" stories. A lady called into a technical support line wanting to know what was wrong with her new computer. The customer service rep asked her several questions to try and ascertain the source of her problems and, in a few minutes, found out that the lady had the mouse on the floor and was trying to push it with her foot like a pedal. She said that it worked with her sewing machine.
>
> My all time favorite story of this type came from the information technology guy at the library where I used to work. He knew a guy who worked information technology at the headquarters of a local textile mill. One of the secretaries called him and told him that the cup holder on the front of her computer wasn't going in anymore. She had been opening the CD drive on the front of her computer and sitting her full can of soda or coffee cup on it to the point that the drive had bent down and wouldn't go back in anymore.

LIS 658, Library Services to Diverse Client Groups, A study of the changing demographic patterns which affect libraries, examination of services, collections and staffing to reflect a variety of cultural, ethnic and racial experiences and needs. An important class especially for those of us working in public libraries. Public libraries are somewhat unusual because we serve almost EVERY aspect of society, every socio-economic class, cultural group, religion and special needs. This is an aspect of our job we dare not forget. A great course but it didn't cover such groups as rednecks, teenagers on Red Bull, and people who like to show their bodies to total strangers.

LIS 603, Last but not least I handed in a portfolio of my projects and works, and in the summer of 2002, graduated with a masters in library and information studies with a 3.6 GPA.

Classes They Should Teach in Library School

1. *Copier and Printer Repair*—"No sir the copier can't print on paper that is laminated."
2. *Hostage Negotiation*—If you are thrown out of the library for looking at inappropriate subject matter on our computers and stomp out cursing, please take your child with you.
3. *Hazmat Certification*—Just the other day a patron's baby had a leaky diaper all over the carpet. What did the parent choose to do? He or she snatched him up and left without telling anybody. Who got to clean this up? The supervisor on duty, that's who. Guess who that was? What I wouldn't have done for one of those hazmat suits. I have talked to librarians who have had grown adults leave surprises of this nature and involving a variety of bodily fluids.
4. *Conflict Resolution*—The fact that you simply don't have any money will not absolve you from paying your overdue fees.
5. *Computer Desk Construction*—Tab A goes into slot B.
6. *Library Facility Repair and Clean Up*—Remember, step one, be nice to maintenance.
7. *Crafts for All Occasions*—I'll just say that children's librarians rock at making crafts out of whatever they find in their desk drawer.
8. *Local Politics and Procedure*—This would be an extremely difficult class seeing as how often the laws and procedures change. I guess step two is to be nice to the commissioners. Some people may say that this is number one but I think I'll stick to my guns.
9. *Heating and Cooling Repair*—STEP ONE: BE NICE TO MAINTENANCE.

Jon's Nine Circles of Library Hell

1. *Tax Season—No, there is no form called a WD-40 (actual reference question).*
2. *First days open after holidays—The only people who aren't coming in are calling.*
3. *Elections—All the taxpayers want you to know who they're voting for, and why.*
4. *Cataloging Class—It's really too terrible to describe.*
5. *Summer Reading—Kids everywhere. It reminds you of the movie theater scene in the movie* Gremlins.
6. *Commissioners Meetings—Your budget is about to be cut, the only decisions to be made are from where and when.*
7. *Cold and Flu Season—There's snot on the computer keyboards and germs everywhere.*
8. *Library Renovation—See chapter 2.*
9. *The G.R.E.—Causing OCD in prospective graduate students everywhere.*

There are a lot of librarians who won't agree with this list, but hey people, it's my book.

5

I Am the Law!

Mr. Duncan left the library while we were still in the temporary facility. There was no goodbye, no party. One morning he was gone, just like that. I realize there were a lot of staff members who were glad to see him gone, or others who couldn't care less. Me, I missed him and still do. Like I said, we always got along. He was a funny guy and I liked working with him. I saw him around town after he left but he would never speak of the library or what happened there. Last I heard he was working at a library in another state; I hope he's still kicking off in the reference department.

The morning that I found out he was gone the other reference librarian and I were called to the director's office. While we were at the temporary location the public access departments were in an old grocery store. The administrative offices and technical services, however, were in a store front a couple of doors down. I remember the long walk down the sidewalk and the nervous, dead feeling that I had in the pit of my stomach. Call me paranoid but I've always made it my goal to stay out of the big bosses' office. It's among some of the strategies that I hold dear to ensure a happy life. (1) Never threaten to sue, quit your job or fight unless you're serious, (2) Don't engage your mouth unless your brain is in gear, and (3) Stay out of Mr. or Ms. Big's office. I always figured that when the director of the county system or, even worse, Human Resources wants you front and center, it's very rarely for a good thing. That belief must have already been ingrained in my psyche because I remember being really nervous and wondering what I could have done to draw the director's ire. When we got there the director greeted us with a very business-like demeanor which did not lesson my anxiety. What he wanted to tell us was that Mr. Duncan was moving on. With Duncan gone the other reference librarian moved up into his spot, no surprise there, he was next in line. From this point I will refer to this librarian, out of respect for his favorite type of automobile, as Mr. Benz. So why was I there? This still made me somewhat nervous. When the director turned to me he smiled. Okay that's a good sign, and told me that some sort of legislation had gone through saying that the law library, which I knew little if not nothing about, had to stay open a set amount of time per week, giving the public as well as those then incarcerated, access to legal materials. This being said, that necessitated a full time position being created to man the law library as well as to assist in certain duties (those that I was already doing) at the public library. That full-time, permanent, salaried position, with benefits was being offered to me. When the director asked if I would accept the position he had hardly gotten the word "do" out when I hit him with a barrage of yesses that could have dropped an elephant. No more passing up opportunities for this guy.

Remember, I had hardly heard of the law library, and that was only when someone had called and asked for the phone number. I had to look high and low for it, and before I had gotten back to the phone the caller had hung up. So, you can understand how this job offer was right out of the blue, and a blessing, because it made it possible for the plans my fiancée and I had—to get married—to progress.

As it turns out, the law library was a very small, closet-sized facility at the County Courthouse. It was housed there, but maintained by the library. The courthouse was across the street from the library building, but when I took over the law library, we were still in the temporary facility and I had to travel halfway across town.

> The courthouse that was in place when I started at the law library had been in use since 1920 and before that it was a block over just behind where the library building presently stood. A few years later a realty office would be built on that corner and was created in a style to resemble the earlier courthouse. A great story that I heard about in the Genealogy Room concerned the old courthouse and was given to me by a patron. We had a framed copy of a photograph of the old courthouse which he brought up to the desk. He told me that he had seen a picture of that same courthouse where the camera had been a little farther from the building so it showed some of the area to either side. He said that there was a tree just beside the courthouse building, that someone had been hanged in that tree and that the body was still hanging from one of the tree limbs. My grandfather also told my father that when he was a young boy he saw someone tied to a post and horse whipped there. Did these stories really happen this way? Maybe so, my grandfather was an honest man, so I don't

doubt it. I didn't know the other guy but again, it's a good story and it was another time. I have no doubt that things like this really went on.

Up until I took it over, the law library had been overseen by a part-time employee who was sort of a handyman/jack-of-all trades and the law library was not at the top of the list of things that demanded his attention. I believe the job of law librarian was created with me in mind, of which I am eternally grateful.

At first I spent three hours a day at the law library and the rest of the day was spent at reference. At first my time at the law library was pretty busy. The place hadn't been very well taken care of, so there was a lot of filing, the shelves were beyond full and books were stacked along the baseboards of every wall; it was almost like being at those Sumerian libraries I spoke of several chapters ago. I was able to catch up on the filing, cancel subscriptions to some of the little used materials and generally clean up. I guess in the grand scheme of things the law library wasn't that big of a deal, but to me it was, and I jumped into it with both feet; I guess I must have seemed like the library alternative to Barney Fife. As the work calmed down I was able to develop an organizational system, a card catalog of sorts, a binder to help locate a particular work. I also set about chasing down some of the books that had been taken out and not returned. The general public wasn't allowed to check out the materials, but could use the materials in the library. The only people allowed to check the materials out were officers of the court, attorneys, clerks, judges and the like and a great deal of these people would take something out and forget they had it, even though they were asked to bring it back in five days. It shouldn't come as a surprise to anyone that legal materials have to be updated fairly often, and a couple of times I had an attorney ask me why a certain publication wasn't updated when he still had it checked out at the time. I stomped into many an office in my quest to retrieve the law library's books, Barney Fife on patrol. I did go into one guy's office and found a lot of our books that I had been looking for, stacked in a corner. They were covered in cobwebs and the spiders were dead, so I could deduce that they had been there awhile and hadn't been used.

"Oh, are we the worst?" The secretary chirped as I was carrying them out. I didn't have a witty comeback for that, or one that wouldn't have gotten me in some serious trouble.

One of the first things that I did for the law library was to purchase a computer and convert some of the larger library services, some of whom could be one hundred volumes or more, to CD-ROM, which was the pinnacle of technology at that time. As is the case with every library, but especially so for such a small library, space was a major issue. At the time I started it looked like the law library would have exploded if you would have added one more volume. When I converted those subscriptions from print to CD-ROM, that took literally dozens of volumes and put them into a space the equivalent of a corner mailbox, when you count the computer, printer, the computer desk and the peripherals. One problem that I did not foresee was the reaction from some of the attorneys. Some did not like the fact that they could not get a book on these subjects, but would have to settle for a printout. Eventually, the grumbling did die down and I offered to teach anyone who wanted to learn how to use these services. Many attorneys came in to get their instruction, but the older ones, who were the most vocal critics, sent their secretaries.

The law library could be an interesting place because it was in the courthouse between two courtrooms and right beside a waiting room. I got to see a judge, clad in his black robes lean out of a men's room window and throw a roll of toilet paper at a bailiff. I also saw a couple of attorneys at a water fountain pouring water onto one of their ties to see if it was really stain proof. Remember ladies and gentlemen, these were the staff members, the public who came to the courthouse were a whole different ballgame. People would hang around out in the hall outside the library and if the door was open they would regularly walk through with nary a word for yours truly, and then leave again without even saying hello or goodbye. The door had a combination lock on it and a lot of times when it was closed a teenager on his way to or from juvenile court would start pushing the buttons like he was playing Nintendo, giggling like a wild man as if this were the funniest thing that had ever happened in the history of funny things, not realizing that another prospective comedian had done it not five minutes before.

The law library had to be open a certain number of hours a week to give the general public access to the materials contained therein. Most of the time when people did come in to use the library the transactions were pretty non-descript. One time, however, a bearded guy came in with a briefcase and introduced himself with a firm handshake. He had in mind becoming some sort of legal mind and offering his services to "the common man." I helped him as best I could but I had a hard time understanding specifically what he wanted. To tell the truth I didn't understand it enough to put it into words here. As I look back on it I'm not really sure if he had a concrete idea of what he wanted, but after a few minutes looking at some of the books he asked if court was going on next door.

"Yes, I think so," I said and he promptly stood up and left the room, leaving the young woman who had come with him there with me, so we stared at each other for a good fifteen minutes before he came in, sat down and started studying the books again. Within seconds a few of the bailiffs came in and while a couple walked the guy and his lady friend out another questioned me as to who I was, why I was here, if I knew the other fellow and whether or not the law library was open to the public. Apparently the guy walked into a juvenile court proceeding, which is supposed to be closed to the public and started asking people questions. Then he got up and walked out. I never saw the guy again so I can't say if he became the legal mind he wanted to be or if he spent time in jail.

Another time I was sitting at the computer in the law library meeting room which offered me a complete view of most of the hallway outside. The door to the waiting room opened and a very shapely, well dressed young lady stepped into the hallway, oblivious of my presence nearby and stood with her back to me looking out the window onto the parking lot outside. As I watched she reached behind her and pulled up the back of her skirt revealing some very thin pantyhose, a very shapely backside and a pair of panties that barely covered it. She began adjusting her panty hose with one hand when I very loudly cleared my throat to make my presence known. I looked back toward the computer's screen and could hear high heels on the tile floor stepping very quickly down the hall back toward the waiting room door.

6

The Future Is Now

The next few months literally flew by with me getting married, getting settled in at the law library, and then as soon as I was back from my honeymoon, we started moving back to our permanent, newly renovated location. Was the move any easier? Not by much, if any, but I think it helped that we knew what to expect, even if the physical labor was in no way lessened.

The first day that we were open in the new location, there was a lot of fanfare, a great deal of excitement from the staff and a lot of praise from the patrons, with one exception. One of the many changes made to the new library was that one entrance was closed and sealed off so there could be only one entrance for the sake of security. With one entrance, security gates were installed so that when somebody walked through them with a book they had not checked out, an alarm was supposed to sound. Remember that metal strip that I put in my roommate's book bag? Same principle. As the morning progressed a rather perturbed looking elderly gentleman could be seen scratching on the glass where the rear entrance used to be. When a library employee went to the window and waved him around the building he stomped in that direction, and when he made it inside he unloaded on Mr. Benz because of the confusion over the rear entrance. Apparently it was not enough that the sidewalk did not lead to that section of the building anymore and that there were no handles to open that section of glass, this patron wanted a sign to inform him where the new entrance was and wanted to file an additional complaint that by moving the entrance it caused him to walk further, despite the fact that the new one was mere feet from the main parking lot. Benz tried to explain the reasoning behind the single entrance and the justification for moving it, but the patron was having none of it.

"Just make a sign!" He screamed and stomped out.

It seemed like we had barely moved into the new building when Mr. Benz and the director began talking about automation. That is, we were to go from the old stamp and card system to an automated one, which is the norm in libraries these days. I think everybody around 30 or older can remember the way libraries used to manage their collections. You would go to the library and if you had to look for a particular book or similar product, you would go to those big wooden card catalogs (you remember I mentioned them in the story concerning my first difficult patron.) They had row upon row of little drawers that were filled with little cards that contained all the information you needed to find what you were looking for. All of those cards were held in place by long metal rods which were screwed into the front of the drawer and ran the length of them. Don't ask how I know, but these rods are really fun to sword fight with and they hurt like hell if you get whacked with them. One time a patron pulled the drawer out too far so the drawer came completely out. Instead of holding onto the drawer they just let it go, so it hit the floor sending cataloging cards everywhere. After the patron was helped I asked Mr. Duncan what to do about it and he said to send it to technical services and let them deal with it.

Automating the library involved setting up the hardware and software, which I was not involved with. Then every book in the county system had to have a barcode placed on it and it had to be scanned into the system. Let me say that again. EVERY BOOK IN THE COUNTY, not every book in the main library, EVERY BOOK IN THE COUNTY, which involved a total of six libraries, HAD TO HAVE A BARCODE PLACED ON IT AND IT HAD TO BE SCANNED INTO THE SYSTEM!

It was physically and mentally exhausting and felt a lot like the building renovation part 2. One day we were all working at one of the county's branch libraries. We were working at a fevered pitch and the director was trying to get the attention of a library employee named Linda. "Linda," he said. When she didn't respond he called a little louder, "Linda!" Still nothing and Linda was standing just a couple of feet from him. "LINDA!" he said and she finally turned her head and looked at him somewhat confused. "Are you okay?" "Yes I am," she said. "This has so stressed me out, I forgot my name." Now Linda is a very intelligent, mature woman, so if she forgot her name you can really tell how much automating the library can take out of you. The first thing a patron said to us when we opened to the public? "It's about time ya'll got back to work."

The automation system made things so much easier not only for our library but for libraries in general. That sort of system is standard in libraries today and I don't think that you will hear a librarian say that they hearken back to the manual way of checking people out or that they would give up the computer system for the little wooden drawers filled with index cards. I should say that there are perhaps librarians who long for the aesthetics of little wood and brass drawers filled with index cards, because I knew of several librarians who have old card catalogs in their homes either as functional drawers or to simply look at.

From automation it was just a hop, skip and a jump to Internet access, which has probably changed libraries more than any other single thing in recent memory. This is just my opinion, however, and I'm sure that people will disagree, but in the time that I have been working in libraries I can almost separate time into B.I., before Internet, and A.I., after Internet. That's how important a factor that I believe it is.

The origins of the Internet can be traced all the way back to Sputnik, which was launched by the Soviet Union on October 4, 1957. Sputnik I was the first artificial satellite. It was twenty-three inches in diameter, it weighed 183 pounds and it took about 90 minutes to orbit Earth. By contrast, modern communications satellites can weigh up to six tons and be the size of a small school bus. One of the United States' responses to Sputnik was to establish the Advanced Research Projects Agency or ARPA. In 1969, ARPA created the ARPAnet to transfer research from one computer to the other, among 4 separate terminals. ARPAnet was a predecessor to the Internet. During the late seventies, Vinton Cerf created what would come to be called "Transmission Control Protocol," or TCP. This allowed all those small closed networks to communicate with each other. In 1991 another programmer named Tim Berners-Lee introduced the World Wide Web, an Internet network that was not just a way to send files back and forth but also served as a web of computer networks that allowed users to retrieve whatever information they wanted, and thus the Digital Age was born.

Of course it's also a double edged sword for libraries, just as is to society in general. As librarians the Internet gives us access to huge amounts of information. Questions that could not be answered 20 years ago now can be these days, and reference transactions that would take an hour or more can be answered in mere minutes. There are subscription services that we can offer our patrons that let them do their résumé, download music and e-books and even learn other languages offered over the Internet. Let's face it, if we were to lose the Internet tomorrow it would be way harder to adapt to living without it than it was to adapt to it.

On the other hand, when libraries started offering Internet access to their patrons, the demographic of people coming into the library changed dramatically. B.I. library patronage was largely, but not wholly, limited to families, older people and kids doing work for school. The Internet brought in more single men, homeless/transients and the mentally ill. Is this solely because of the Internet? No, not necessarily. Like I said previously, public libraries have always been opened to anyone and assisted everyone. Is this completely bad? No, again public libraries are called that for a reason, but it has changed the way libraries operate and presented situations that they didn't have to deal with in the early nineties, B.I., when I first started. The challenging part is that these sectors of society bring with them their own challenges, and librarians have to be ready to meet those challenges.

When we first started offering public Internet access at the library it was pretty much wide open. Patrons came up to the desk, we signed them in and the computer was theirs for as long as they wanted it. At that time chat rooms were all the rage, they were the only social media at the time and we had patrons who would, if allowed, sit in front of them for literally hours. No breaks for food, no breaks to go to the bathroom, no nothing. I have been told that this unwillingness to leave the terminal has made for some rather messy situations in the chairs these people were sitting in. One young woman who came in our library was named Terrie, although I can't remember if that was her first or last name. She would arrive wearing the uniform for a local fast food establishment and would sit down for a chat room marathon. I don't know if she was just coming from work, but if that was where she was headed, she would never get there, because for hours she would chat with a big Cheshire cat-like grin stretched across her face. It seemed like there was always the same guy just a couple of seats from her. He was there just as long and always had the same kind of smile. I always wondered if they were chatting with each other and didn't know it and what they were saying to each other.

There was a couple that would come in around about the same time. They were both large people, so I always privately called them "two tons of fun." They were supposedly engaged, but while they would come in together, they would sit apart and chat with other people. I know for a fact that at least the guy spent a great deal of time in chat rooms that were of a sexual nature, but since he wasn't displaying any obscene pictures on the screen, he wasn't breaking any rules, so we didn't say anything. The funny part was that he had some sort of nervous tic where his head would bob up and down violently like those toy birds that would drink out of a glass of water. The more excited he got the more his head would bob, so if he were chatting with some hot young thing, again, not his fiancée, and locked in a really steamy conversation, it looked like he was going into convulsions or head banging at some heavy metal concert. There was news that the woman had met someone through one of these chat rooms and was meeting them at a motel in Virginia. I can't say what happened with that rendezvous or the marriage because the couple eventually stopped coming, as did Miss Terrie and the man who seemed to hover around her, but as I stated before, when one nutty patron leaves there will be another one to take his place.

In libraries, as with society in general, technology has changed a lot and I think that public libraries have changed more than a lot of professions. When I started in libraries the be all and end all was CD-ROM technology. We had several programs on CD at the reference desk, and if a patron wanted to use them they had to come and retrieve them at the desk and take them to one of our two public computers. This was when 5¼ floppy disks were still relevant. For those of you who remember floppy disks, they were probably 3½. 5¼s were bigger and a lot thinner but couldn't hold as much as 3½s. The drives, or slots they fit in on the front of the computer, were roughly the size of the CDs and it seemed like once a week a patron would get one of the CDs, and instead of putting it into the slot that was labeled "CD" they would peel it out of the thick plastic case that it was supposed to remain in and cram it into the 5¼ slot. When that happened the then head of reference, Mr. Duncan—he of the short temper and bad balance—would have to take the shell of the CPU, the main part of the computer, completely off and pry out the CD. This would happen at least once a week, sometimes more, and was sure to raise said librarian's blood pressure.

In the time since then, libraries have automated and moved from paper and ink systems of checking out to automated systems, most of which depend on barcodes for the identification of the patron and the materials they are checking in and/or out. The methods used in reference, that is to answer our patron's questions, have changed as the Internet consistently proves itself as a faster, cheaper and more space conscious alternative to shelves of reference books.

I will take this moment to say that several librarians I've talked to see the book—that is the codex format, pages linked at the spine and pressed between two covers—as a form that is on the way out; that within our lifetime the book as we have seen it for our entire lifetimes will eventually cease to exist. To this theory I must respectfully disagree. Despite all the advantages that technology has, we will still continue to see entire stores, their shelves lined with books. There are several reasons why I would say that. First, let's talk price. I can still buy a book for less than a dollar. True, many libraries have free e-book downloads, but what about the reader? The device to read them on can still be quite expensive. Remember, money talks. Also there's simplicity. With a book you simply have to sit down and open it. With a reader it has to be turned on. With a book you don't need a power source or you don't need to make sure your batteries are charged. You just need enough light to see it. With an e-reader the book has to be downloaded, it's a lot more involved than popping open a paperback. Also, one thing people need to realize before they go all gaga over technology, is that not everybody is capable of using such devices. Some are not capable mentally and some would just rather not. To quote a grad school professor of mine: "The absolute last thing I want to do in my few remaining years on this earth is to learn how to use some damn fool machine!" In a nutshell, and this is to librarians specifically, don't be too hasty to push the technological alternative when doing it old school could be just as quick and easy in answering the patron's question. If you know you might be surfing around on the Internet for awhile, just go blow the dust off a reference book and use it.

There were a lot of bugs that had to be worked out when free access to the Internet became a library staple. How do you police what sites people visit? Is there an age limit? How do you limit their time on the computer, or do you? Do you filter? One further question that immediately came up when libraries entered the Digital Age was how to handle the problem of pornography.

I don't have evidence of this, but I would be willing to bet that porn has been around for as long as people have. As soon as someone drew two stick figures in a compromising position on a cave wall, pornography was born. The first documented account of modern pornography goes back to the 16th century and the Italian Renaissance. In 1524 Marcantonio Raimondi published sixteen sexually explicit engravings by artist Giulio Romano entitled, *I Modi*. At the time the engravings were considered so scandalous that Pope Clement VIII placed Raimondi in prison for a year. Just a couple of years later, Italian author Pietro Aretino wrote two pornographic novels, *I Sonetti Lussuriosi* in 1527 and *Ragionamenti* from 1534 to 1536. *I Sonetti Lussuriosi* combined Aretino's X-rated poems with the engravings from *I Modi*. The *Ragionamenti* was an extension of *I Sonetti Lussuriosi* and documented a conversation between two prostitutes. For decades these two works were it, where perverted stories were concerned. Most new pornographic works were either direct copies or cheap knockoffs. One example is *L'École des filles*, which was almost a direct copy of *Ragionamenti*, but many consider it the beginning of the iconic French pornography, which ballooned after the French Revolution when print sources previously reserved for the upper class became available to the common man.

Pornography is nothing if it's not adaptable. It seems that every time there is some sort of technological breakthrough, porn has used it to get T & A to more and more people. As printing costs continued to fall, pornographic material continued to expand its market, and in 1837 there were more than fifty pornographic shops in London. In 1839 Louis Daguerre sold the rights to his daguerreotype—a form of photography where a single image was imposed onto a metal plate—to the French government who proceeded to send the technology around the world. The earliest known pornographic daguerreotype is an 1846 exposure (you'll have to use your imagination as to what it was) which is housed at the Kinsey Institute. The collodion process replaced the daguerreotype in 1851 and made it possible to produce better detailed pictures on a glass plate negative, which made it easier to produce multiple prints. This led to the industrialization of photography, as well as pornography, and in the early 1850s 40 percent of the photographs registered for sale in Paris were nudes. Production also increased in Britain and the United States, and the distribution of pornography started occurring at train stations, barber shops, bars, fairs, pushcarts and theaters. On March 22, 1895, the Lumière Brothers projected their first black and white film to an audience in Paris using the film technologies devised by Henry M. Reichenbach, Thomas Edison and William Kennedy Dickson as well as Charles-Émile Reynaud. This soon popularized a simple but very popular form of cinema. The very next year a French film entitled *Le Coucher de la Mariée* became the first pornographic film. The "stag film" remained popular until the 1970s when feature length adult movies replaced the poor quality, illegal one reel stag films. Throughout the 20th century pornographic magazines continued to develop from the Tijuana Bibles of the 1920s to *Playboy* (1953), *Penthouse* (1965) and *Hustler* in 1974. In the late 1980s the availability of the VCR made it possible for people to purchase pornography in a more discrete fashion and view it in the privacy of their own homes, which leads us back to where our X-rated journey started. The Internet has once again revolutionized pornography, as it is now available free of charge and viewable pretty much anywhere on computers, tablets and even phones. This, if you ask me, would make it possible for people to stay at home in the comfort of their own domicile and watch smut in private rather than subject an entire reference desk to whatever fetish you happen to be into at the time.

If you work in a public library setting long enough—and actually work with the public—you will catch some guy looking at pornography. And let's face it, 99 times out of a hundred it's a guy. One thing I will add is that a great deal of the guys I've caught went to said nudie page largely out of curiosity. They saw a link that came up on Google or some similar kind of search engine and thought they could click on it, get an eye full and then back out again before anyone noticed. The trouble is, when you try and exit one of these pages, you may simply be redirected to another porn page, and when you try and leave that one you are directed to yet another one. The peeper finds himself stuck on a porn page and can't get out. You can tell one of these guys because he is sitting there mindlessly surfing the Internet, minding his own business, a million mile stare stretched across his face like so many of the other people around him. Then he gets really interested in something and he leans in, putting his face closer to the monitor as he reads through all the obscene words on the link. Then he glances to the people on either side of him to make sure he isn't being watched and clicks the mouse. His eyes get a little bigger as he gets his jollies. Then he clicks again and tries to exit the page. When he figures out that he can't, his eyes start to dart around from person to person and then up to the reference desk. Then he starts to click frantically, almost like he's trying to put his finger through the mouse. That's when I very casually walk around the reference desk, take my time, maybe say hello to a couple of the regulars and slowly make my way to where he is sitting, still pounding the mouse with his finger. He gets a warning but I always let him get back on the computer, lesson learned. One guy who tried this even ran out rather than get caught.

One time one of my co-workers was working at the reference desk and a woman who had been on the Internet approached her and very loudly told her that the man who was sitting next to her was looking at porn. The co-worker looked toward the Internet computers and everyone who was using one, in unison, looked up, looked at my co-worker and then at the seat next to where the woman had been sitting. There was a man, about twentyish, on the computer. He had his jacket on his lap and his hand was moving rhythmically beneath it. Before any action could be taken, the man jumped up and ran for the door.

I've only semi-directly dealt with someone once who had the gall to argue with the librarians after being busted for pornography. The guy was actually the ex-husband of a friend of my mother's, and a co-worker had made him log off of Playboy.com, not quite as obscene as some sites, but a violation of policy nonetheless. After he had logged off he stopped by the lending desk and asked one of the other librarians why he couldn't "look at nudes."

"Sir," the librarian told him, "those were not nudes." She was apparently appalled at the man's inability to tell the difference between Botticelli's *Venus* and *Hot Moms on the Beach*. I have heard a couple of librarians, not ones who have a lot of experience in a public setting, say that library patrons should be allowed to look at pornography all they want to. Apparently there are a great many conversations in library schools saying that looking at sodomy on a publicly owned computer is somehow covered under the First Amendment. Others have thrown in the belief that the definition of porn, as given under state law, is too vague, and because we can't completely define and classify porn, people can look at *www.asiandelights.com* on a public computer in front of God and everybody. For these people I have included a list at the end of the chapter which gives ways that a librarian, or anyone else for that matter, can tell whether it's porn or it's not. No offense to those who see things this way but I do have to respectfully disagree on this viewpoint.

First off, everyone reading this knows what porn is, no matter what the specific definition is in the law books. People know what porn is when they see it and it has no place being viewed in a public library. Do people have the right to look at porn if they want to? Sure they do, in the privacy of their own home or some similar place where people who have no urge to see such things don't have to be subjected to it. To quote my mother-in-law, "where my nose starts your freedom ends." Additionally, porn is not something that you need for your existence. You need a certain amount of education. You need to work on your resumé to find a job. I can even see that you need to check your e-mail or Facebook to communicate with friends and family that you might not otherwise contact or even communicate with at your place of employment. You don't require porn to live.

For those budding librarians who still think that people should be allowed to view such material and have a dream of making porn freedom a policy in their library one day as a blow toward unfettered intellectual freedom, let me put it to you this way. There are people who may come into your library called commissioners. They make some of the decisions involving your library and they control the purse strings. Even if they don't physically come in, there is a likelihood that another group who are known as library patrons who are also known as taxpayers may be more than happy to tell the commissioners if they see such things in a library that their taxes support. If these commissioners find out that you are allowing people to openly look at pornography in a public library using publicly funded equipment, this could affect the library the next time it's time to lay out the budget for the next year. Oh yeah, and regarding your career, you are done. Done, meaning go directly to McDonald's and put in your application.

Porn and other such undesirable material that is all too easy accessed via the Internet is, I guess, the reason that libraries are required by federal law to filter their public computers. I do have to say that filters are of no use in keeping porn off public computers. Filters are counter-productive. First, anyone with the technological savvy of a three-year-old can get around a filter. One way that pornography comes in these days is Facebook and other social media. Another drawback to filters is that they block legitimate sites and keep people from researching legitimate topics. I'll give you an example. One day at my previous place of employment we helped a young lady do a research paper on ex vice-president Dick Cheney because her school's computers blocked sites mentioning him because of his first name. Filters don't block pictures. They don't see pictures, they block words. So if a porn site doesn't have those select words, those images we are speaking of will get through anyway.

My policy regarding the content that patrons are allowed to view would be to leave it up to the librarian on duty. If the patron wants to dispute his or her decision, then it can be referred to a supervisor. It would be great if we lived in a world where people would have the discretion that if there's any question about the image, they just wouldn't pull it up, but that's not the case. If you work in a public library long enough it's something that you will have to deal with.

I have to wonder that, as time passes, if more and more places will start offering Wi-Fi or if our urban areas will turn into one big hot spot. If that's the case, just offering Internet access won't be enough. I think where libraries really make a difference where access to technology is concerned is through instruction and training for the public. As I said before, one thing many people and institutions—including most businesses and our government—forget, is that even though people have access to the Internet, they're not always capable of using it. That's where the library comes in. I remember a really early incident involving a local employer, a chain of grocery stores. They made it a policy that everyone who applied at one of their stores from manager to bagger had to apply online. They no longer accepted paper applications. Well, some of the people who apply at grocery stores not only don't have access to the Internet but don't know how to use it. They rightfully came to the library, but it took sitting down with the patrons for several minutes at a time. The thing that made things even more complicated is that this company wouldn't communicate with prospective employees by mail or even by phone. They required an e-mail address, which meant that we had to help the patron, who had never used a computer before, not only set up an e-mail address and apply for the job, but check it periodically. Even though we were glad to offer the access and the assistance, it got to the point where one of my co-workers contacted the company to inform them of how hard it was making it for prospective employees. I don't think that she ever heard back.

For a few years I taught basic computer classes for our patrons from mouse basics to advanced Internet searching. Learning to use the mouse is a lot different than other skills it takes to use a computer. The rest of the skills involve memory. You need to know what, where and how to type something. The skills in using the mouse are physical, it takes hand-eye coordination. People of my generation and those generations that followed it developed this hand-eye coordination through video games, so learning how to use a mouse became pretty much second nature. If you are much older than me or if you didn't play video games as much as the rest of us, it might be a great deal harder. One thing I had to overcome in teaching these classes was that people wanted to pinch the mouse between their thumb and forefinger like it was hot and they were scared of getting burned. It took a few minutes to get people to hold the mouse so that the curved top rested against their palm, which is the correct method. There were a couple of great mouse tutorials online that I used for this type of instruction, but one of the best ways of teaching mouse basics was to let people play the Solitaire game that was included in most of the Windows programs. There are also a couple of sites you can access that give you online jigsaw puzzles that you can solve with the drag and drop method and further polish your mouse skills.

The rest of the classes involved finding your way around the keyboard, how to enter a URL, how to print, first using a print preview, how to send and receive an e-mail and how to search using a search engine or directory. For the more advanced class I pretty much went on what the patron wanted to learn, since the classes were usually small, one or two people. We covered how to find directions using Google maps and another class centered on looking for jobs and typing a résumé using the résumé program the library had purchased through a subscription. We even had another class where I helped a couple of patrons set up an eBay account, although this was in the same class as another subject because all I could help them do was set up an account. I could not assist them in putting in personal information such as account numbers.

It was extremely rewarding to see people, mostly older patrons, come in with apprehensions about any sort of technology and before long they were e-mailing their grandchildren their Christmas photos and shopping online. It was one of the more rewarding aspects of my career. One older lady in a class on e-mail made perhaps one of the funnier statements that I have ever heard on the subject. She was the only person in the class so I could customize it somewhat for her. She had informed me that she already had an e-mail account, but that she had questions. When I asked her what I could help her with she told me that she wanted to know how to block the spam that she had been getting. "I have been getting offers for products to enlarge something that I don't have!" she told me.

How to Tell If a Patron Is Viewing Porn as Opposed to a Nude

1. If the image involves a motorcycle or a boa constrictor it's porn.
2. If any of the people in the image have tattoos it might be porn.
3. If there are any piercings, especially on parts of the body that you couldn't see if the person were wearing a bikini, it's porn.
4. If plastic and/or latex is involved it's porn.
5. If anything is inserted into anything, it's porn.

7

Does Your Family Tree Fork?

My dad told me something on my first day as a full time employee at the library. "Stay busy," he said. "Nobody wants to see you standing around. If you can't find enough to do, you ask somebody." Of course this is also the same person who told me that one of the things he learned in the army was never, never, volunteer for anything. I did try and follow his first piece of advice and was never one to claim that "it's not in my job description" when I was asked to do something. I will say, however, that this mantra has served to get me some of the jobs that nobody else wanted.

My father has always had a rather unusual way of teaching me life's little lessons. One summer when I was home from college he came home with an old fashioned mule plow in the back of his truck. That is one of those plows that you would hitch behind a team of mules and plow with in the days before tractors. He got me to help him unload it and then carry it to a field that he rented to grow vegetables. Once it was there we hitched it behind my father's tractor, and then while he pulled it back and forth across the field, I attempted to steer it. Now picture this in your mind, stereotypical old man in a straw hat driving the tractor and pulling the plow and young kid with long hair and ripped jeans trying to steer it. One thing that I learned really quickly was that these plows do not stay up and go straight on their own. You have to hang on and force them to do so. If the blade hits a stick, a rock or even a compacted section of earth, it will jump and the long wooden handles you are holding on to try and steer it, might come up into your chin, your stomach, maybe even your groin. It was not a pleasant experience and after we were done and I was lying on the ground in a fetal position I asked my Dad why we just did that. He had a tractor that could plow perfectly. What was the point of bringing in the antique?

"I just wanted you to see how we used to do it," he responded. What he meant was that he wanted to show me how good I had it and this was a valuable lesson. That's why I never complained about having to be on the reference desk for longer than two hours or carrying a big box of donated books from a patron's car to the library or cleaning the leakage from a kid's diaper because the parent simply snatched him up and left, leaving his mess all over the library's floor. Okay, maybe I did complain about that last one, but what I'm trying to get across is that working in a library is not a hard job. Yes, it can be challenging and taxing but physically hard? Not as a rule. That's what I learned being dragged across that field all those years ago. I learned what truly hard work is and library work isn't it.

When I started at the library it was around early April, and at least once a day Mr. Duncan would walk up to me and through clinched teeth say, "Tax forms!" I didn't understand his irritation, other than the fact that he was always irritated, and after he was gone I found myself with too little to do and went to Mr. Benz and asked him if he had anything that I could do. He gave me a smile reminiscent of Kaa, the snake in the movie *The Jungle Book*, and told me that somebody needed to manage the tax forms. It didn't take long after I had taken them over to realize why Mr. Duncan had been so vexed by the mere existence of them.

When you manage the distribution of the tax forms in a public library setting, there are two main problems that stand in the way of doing an acceptable job. First is the fact that there are so many types of them. I went onto the I.R.S. website to see if I could find out how many different types of federal tax forms there are. The first answer I found was 1,120. Another site said that there are 900. I don't know how many there were at the time I am speaking about, but there were still a multitude of different types of forms, which leads the librarian to try and figure out which and how many forms we are supposed to provide. Remember, there is the eternal problem of space. There isn't enough space to display and store that many kinds of forms, so we always just kept the very basic ones in addition to a large white binder that held copies of forms so the patron could photocopy them. The thing was, even the binder didn't have every type, so sometimes a patron left unsatisfied with a 1 800 number to the IRS instead of the form he was looking for. The other hindrance to effective tax form distribution has to do with the fact that people can't seem to follow simple instructions. Remember, we didn't have that many forms on hand because we didn't have that much space. The problem was that people wouldn't just take one or two forms as they needed them, they would sometimes take a dozen, maybe more and it seemed like only a couple of days after I had gotten in one shipment, I would have to order more which would take at least a week to get there. People would just have to be turned away or make a copy out of the binder. The biggest culprits of this practice were people who did tax preparation. I'm not talking about people who work for Liberty Tax Service, or H & R Block. I'm talking about the people who do taxes out of their house and seem to be unwilling to pick up the phone and order their own forms. They would just pick them up by the handful at the library. I put up signs saying "please do not take more than 3 tax forms per person" in increasing font sizes and brighter font colors, but I never could get people to comply. These days we don't need the binder, any form can just be printed off the Internet. It is still customary to keep hard copies on hand, however, and there is always that person who wants their form right then and there, so there is still the problem of how many to order and how much space you have and I'm sure the CEO of Lucky's Tax Preparation and Taxidermy will be in to relieve you of all your 1040s at least once a week.

I actually look pretty good here. You're lucky you can't hear me playing.

One morning as I was in the law library trying to figure out which lawyer had which law book, Mr. Benz came in giving me another Kaa smile.

"There's a need for help in the Genealogy Room," he said. "Are you up for it?"

"Sure," I said, and we set about adjusting my schedule to fit in time in the law library, reference and the Genealogy Room, our local history and genealogy department.

For those of you without a dictionary, genealogy is the study and the tracing of your family tree. That is, you go from yourself to your parents, to their parents, to their parents and so on and so on and so forth. The lady who supervised the

Genealogy Room said that she heard a little boy say that the Genealogy Room was full of "a lot of mee maws and pee paws."

Our county's historical collection was largely the baby of one lady who served as county historian for 36 years. She had a collection of papers that dealt with our county's history and maintained regular office hours in the county courthouse and then later at the public library. She was instrumental in founding the county historical society and known throughout the state of North Carolina for her efforts as a historian and preservationist.

As it turns out, the Grande Dame of the County Library system, who would serve as director of the library system for 28 years, was an ardent historian herself. She made it a point to have the first lady's collection and used it to set up the local history and genealogy department, which started out in a room little bigger than a closet. The collection started to grow right off the bat, and by the time I got there, the collection had grown to 5,000 and that's in addition to microfilm, photographs and pamphlet files.

I had some exposure to genealogy since my aunt had traced our family's tree and had shared that information with me. When she died, a while after I was done in the Genealogy Room, she left me all her collected information. I can't say that I am as big a fan of history and genealogy as some people, but it seems as though I am always being directed into situations where I am involved in it. The first Farlow in our line to come to America was Thomas who arrived in the New World from England in 1620. Thomas was a member of the House of Burgesses, which was the first assembly of elected officials in North America. The Farlows settled around Lancaster, Pennsylvania. The first in the family to relocate to Piedmont North Carolina was a couple named Ruth and Nathan, who settled in Randolph County, and we've been there ever since. A large majority of the Farlows in this section of the state come from Ruth and Nathan through their 4 sons. My specific line came through George. Once they were in North Carolina my ancestors did nothing. No war heroes, no criminals, no nothing. The only unusual story I was able to find in our line was that one of our ancestors reached under a bush for a watermelon and was bitten by a rattlesnake. Oh and I'm supposedly connected to the Smothers Brothers on my mother's side. I'm not sure if that second tidbit of information is an actual proven fact or if it's anything to brag about, but I've been told that my whole life.

I did get a copy of some research from a Farlow who actually went to England and poked around a little. He was able to find one of the first instances where a variation on the name Farlow was recorded. It was spelled "dePharlawe" and if this person is in our line, and I hope he is, there is another person connected to him who was a Danish king who laid siege to London for six months.

7. Does Your Family Tree Fork?

Alas, I have no documentation, so maybe there is a connection, maybe there isn't.

You noticed that I made mention of our line or "the first Farlow in our line." That's one of the many things I learned while I worked in the Genealogy Room. A family is made up of lines, that is, just because your name is Washington doesn't mean that you are a descendant of the father of our country. There are a great many people named Washington who are not related to each other or George Washington. They are from different lines of the Washington family name. That's important because I believe that a great many people start tracing their family tree with stars in their eyes. They want to find that historical figure. They want to find that hero, that celebrity, that member of royalty. The thing is, just because a great person has your name doesn't mean they are in any way related to you. One instance where this always comes into play is in the example of family crests. Everybody wants to find their family crest. These days you can pay money to have it found for you, if you don't want to do it yourself. You can get family crests framed so you can put them on your wall. You can have them engraved on rings and wrist watches. You can get them on t-shirts and some people even have them tattooed onto their skin. Does that crest represent your specific line or family? Maybe so, there's a definite chance, but then again maybe not. Once I was told that if a family was important enough to have a crest they stayed where they were and didn't bother to come to the New World. Even if you find a connection with that crest, there has to be documentation. If there is no documentation then what you are telling people is just a story.

Why am I going into this? Because many times this can become an issue for the researcher, which becomes an issue for the librarian. You remember those people who start tracing their family tree with stars in their eyes looking for prince so-and-so? Well those people can be quite disappointed when they don't find prince so-and-so. Instead they find Bert the horse thief or they find out that Great-Grandpa Sims's parents were never married. There was a cartoon posted in the back room of the Genealogy Room that illustrates it. The first frame shows a woman walking into the genealogy department and above her head there is a thought bubble with a picture of a man in a robe and crown, royalty. She states, "I love genealogy." In the next frame she is leaving the genealogy room saying, "I hate genealogy." In the thought bubble is a man in the stockade. We need to remember our ancestors weren't perfect just like we're not perfect. If you find something undesirable in your family tree, it is no reflection on you, it means that your ancestors were human. Remember, there are always a couple of nuts hanging on the branches of every family tree. Rodney Dangerfield used to say, "I traced my roots back to a cesspool."

Another thing unusual about some of the people who came into the Genealogy Room, was that when they learned their family came from a particular country or a particular type of people, they started talking about themselves like they were a native of that country or a part of that group. These days a lot of people want to find that they have a Native American in their line so they can say that they are part Indian. I've even talked to people who started referring to themselves as Indian or started referring to "my people." Just because you have a Native American several generations back in your family does not make you Native American. It does not make you part of a tribe. You have no claim to the casino money. My supervisor in the Genealogy Room said that this was unusual because not too long ago people considered it a disgrace to find Indian blood in their family and now it is considered an honor. She always wondered if people would ever start rethinking their views on having African American ancestors. There are still a great many who do not want to find an African American person in their family tree. She wondered if, in a few years, people would consider this an honor as well.

This is also the case when people learn that their ancestors came from another country. They start talking about themselves like they are a native of that country even though they have never set foot on that country's soil. My ancestors came from England, but I am not English. I do not consider myself English. There is a little town in England called Farlow and there is a high end sporting goods store in London called Farlow's. Still, I have never been to England so all I can call myself is just a plain old run of the mill American.

One day one of our regulars walked into the Genealogy Room. I was engrossed in something and had to do a double take as he walked up to the desk where I was sitting. He was decked out in full Scottish regalia. He had the kilt, he had the sporran, the knee socks, the ruffled shirt the coat and the tam. He even had a dirk, an ornate Scottish dagger, stuck into his belt. I asked him if it was Halloween and he proceeded to describe each piece of clothing, even quoting me the price. Apparently the whole outfit cost him a pretty penny. He didn't show me but he confided that he was going against custom and wearing underwear under his kilt. "You know when this tweed rubs up against the end of your penis it hurts." I didn't know what to say, so I asked him what sort of occasion would prompt the purchase of such an outfit. "No special occasion." He dug his thumbs in his belt and puffed his chest out, "I just thought that I would dress to reflect my Scottish heritage."

"Oh I didn't know you were born in Scotland," I said.

"Well, I wasn't, I was born in Greensboro."

"Are your parents from Scotland?"

"No, they came from Rowan County."

"Oh, okay," was all I said. What I wanted to say was, "Then that makes you an American not a Scotsman and that's not a kilt, it's a dress."

One thing I learned within a couple of days of working in the Genealogy Room is that genealogists, or genies as I have heard them called, are an excitable bunch. The first time I was actually cursed at by a patron was by a genealogist who wanted to get into the Genealogy Room just a few minutes early. This aspect of the confrontation is far from unique. I have had people approach me as I was coming to work, knock on the front door, press their faces against the glass, even get irate because they got the hours of operation wrong. The thing that made this patron different was how irate he got and who he was. This particular individual was a local mill owner, quite wealthy and known as a pillar of the community. He was also known for having a volcanic temper. This morning as an employee came in, he came in as well.

"Sir, we will be opening in about five minutes," I said, in my best business-like manner.

"Nah," he sneered, and he motioned for the people waiting with him to come on in as well. "Close enough."

"Sir," I said. "Again, we're not open yet, you'll have to wait."

"It's just a couple of minutes!" he thundered. "You don't have to be an ass about it!" This should end there, but a couple of days later he pitched a fit in the parking lot of a local drug store, which again he was legendary for doing, and dropped dead of a heart attack on the spot. I guess this isn't unheard of because the man was older, but after news had gotten out about his death and our altercation at the library, people were congratulating me on cursing him. You have to feel sorry for someone who is so miserable to be around, that people are happy after they're gone.

Another strange thing that occurred not once or twice, but on multiple occasions, was a strain of paranoia that seemed to infect some of the regulars who came into the Genealogy Room. More than once I have had a Genealogy Room patron come to the conclusion that someone had tampered with the genealogical records contained in our archives or had out and out stolen them. Is this possible? I guess, but still I can't help but think that it would not happen that often. Also, a couple of these individuals thought that the materials were removed, not by someone stealing them for themselves, but as a conspiracy to keep information that might be deemed controversial away from prying eyes. Could this happen? I guess, but I can't really see it being a regular occurrence.

One person who would always make this assumption was a regular who would call constantly and end up just making small talk for minutes or hours, if you let him. He didn't come in that often because of a problem with transportation, but when he did he was always sure to ask, "Are you sure that nobody has taken anything out of these folders and removed them from this room? I know I donated so and so to this collection and it should be in this folder. Somebody has removed it and I want to know who and why." I always carried on a good working relationship with this guy and would assure him that, to my knowledge, nothing had been removed from said folders. He would leave feeling a little better regarding his suspicions but the next time he was in he would go off on the same old tangent. I do have to say, that while I was being truthful that nobody had removed anything from the folders he was speaking of, I know for a fact something had been taken. One of the other librarians in that department told me that one day an older woman was going through some of the files on one of the families, and all of a sudden she became really angry, gathered her things and made for the door waving one of the documents from the folder in front of her face. "This isn't true and I'm taking it out of here!" Even though this was your stereotypical little old lady, the librarian said she was so mad she just let her go.

Another fellow who would often make these claims was a great deal more aggressive in his claims and there were stories of him being thrown out of other libraries and genealogical society meetings as well, but, although he could be combative in the Genealogy Room, he never got that bad. When I dealt with him his concerns always seemed to involve the microfilm. We had newspapers and various other documents, census, birth records, etc., which we had put onto microfilm and could be viewed on a reader. However, the quality of the image on microfilm is limited by the quality of the hard copy image. That is, if the image on newsprint is faded, it will be even more so when you convert it to microfilm. Sometimes if the image is so deteriorated that it won't convert, or won't be visible, the company that converts the documents to microfilm will simply leave that page blank, and maybe put a message apologizing for the deletion in its place. Whenever this second patron would see that, he would go ballistic and start claiming that the government had broken in and purposefully deleted information to somehow hinder his progress in tracing his family tree. This patron would not be denied and could not be convinced that during the night when we were closed, Donald Rumsfeld did not repel through the roof and somehow wipe out microfilm records to keep this person from finding out who his great-great-grand uncle was. The head of the Genealogy Room informed me, after I had left that department, that this particular gentleman was in one day and suddenly jumped up from his chair and ran out. In a few minutes he returned and asked the librarian if she had felt okay. "Yes I feel fine," she said. "Are you okay?" "Well no," the man said. "I was just sitting here working and all of a sudden the top of my head just started burning."

Let me move away from the Genealogy Room to talk about a patron that we were dealing with at reference about that same time. He would call at least once or twice a week and ask for some sort of cryptic piece of information claiming to be working for the FBI. Apparently he worked at a local mill and would call the library while he was on the clock, so while he was on the phone claiming to be a fed his co-workers or supervisors would be yelling at him in the background to get back to work. I always wondered that it was too bad the two patrons—the one who thought he was being harassed by the FBI and the one who thought he was working for the FBI—couldn't cross paths in the library. The entertainment value would have been priceless. I do think that when patrons realize the library is a government institution they assume we're part of a larger government conspiracy. Over the years I've been accused of being involved in plots to bleed people's bank accounts 20 cents at a time and stockpiling tax forms so people wouldn't be able to get theirs and properly file their tax returns.

I do have to admit that it was sort of like stepping into another world when I started in the Genealogy Room. The sources that I had to learn to use in genealogy weren't covered in grad school, so I had to learn them on the fly. I had heard my aunt mention them when she was telling me about our family tree, but how much do kids ever listen to their elders, even when they're trying to tell them about their own flesh and blood? There is even a book in the Genealogy Room on our family and it's the same one that has been in my parents' house since I was old enough to read the cover. There are a lot of books that have been written on the various families in our area, but one thing I learned about them is, before you use information contained in a given book, stop to think who wrote it, where they got their information, do they document their work and is it accurate?

The census is always a tool people are quick to use in tracing the old family stalk. The first federal census took place in 1790 but it wasn't until the 1850 census that the government listed every single person of the household and their occupation, making these records more useful for genealogists and historians. The census takes place every 10 years and is kept under lock and key by the state for 70 years before releasing it to the public. In the Genealogy Room every census would be available on paper and microfilm from 1790 to 1940, that one being released in 2010, with most of the 1890 census missing because of a fire at the nation's capital which destroyed those records. Our Genealogy Room, as well as many others in the state, are a great holding for South Carolina records as well as North Carolina. When General Sherman marched through South Carolina during the Civil War he burned a lot of their records.

The census is very useful, probably the records most used by people when they were tracing their family tree. There were only a couple of things that I thought were funny about them. One was something they shared with a great deal of those old documents. That being that they were composed with some of the most illegible writing that I have ever seen. The lady who headed the Genealogy Room was the best I've ever seen in making out that chicken scratch that whoever they got to be census takers scrawled out across those forms. The other thing that kind of flummoxed me were the liberties that the census takers took with the information the people they were interviewing gave them. You couldn't guarantee the spelling of the surname, or the first name for that matter, by the census because the census takers never seemed to take the time to clarify it. They just wrote it down in the way that they thought it should be written. The same went for race. They just went by how the person looked. A light skinned African American might be put down as a mulatto. A mulatto might be down as Indian. Again, they never bothered to ask. They just looked at them, decided for themselves and wrote it down. Pretty careless for a government document. I don't know what kind of person they got to do this job, but they definitely didn't require an IQ test.

One of the kinds of records I looked over throughout my time in the Genealogy Room was the documents that recorded a child being bound. Let's say that there is a child in the community that is an orphan or whose parents can't afford to take care of them. They can be bound. That is, they can be handed over to a family member or a member of the community. In exchange for their upkeep the child was expected to do work around the house or maybe farm work. When they left the household they repaid the person who they had been bound to with an "article of value" such as livestock. You don't have to think too hard about this to realize what it was. It was basically slavery with a little fancier name. A child was bought by someone and they owned the child until they came to a certain age. Then they had to buy the person they had been owned by something of value before they could be given their freedom again.

One of the more rewarding things I was able to help develop when I was in the Genealogy Room was an index of the obituaries contained in the microfilm copies of our local paper. I started at the first regular papers in 1903 and worked my way up into the early nineties. At first this sounds like a very tedious and dry undertaking, but I found the old newspapers fascinating both in the content and the way the articles were presented. First off, there were things in those papers that I can't see happening with any regularity these days. So many people burned to death because they got too close to the fireplace, especially women when their skirt tails caught fire. Also, countless people were hit by trains. It seemed like this would be pretty hard to do. Trains aren't necessarily quiet. It would be difficult for them to sneak up on you, but nevertheless, it seemed like every couple of months someone would be found dead either on or beside the tracks. The account I will never forget involving a train was one where a drunken man passed out beside the tracks, with his arms laying across one of the rails, and while he was asleep, the train came by and he woke up with no hands. Sounds like something right out of a horror movie.

There were a lot of surprises in the papers back then, because where as papers these days like to at least try and appear non-biased, the writers in those days made their opinions known. I noticed that they did not have very much sympathy for African Americans and if a black person fell upon some sort of tragedy it was inevitably their own fault. Remember, the instances concerning women catching their skirts on fire? I remember reading a couple concerning women who, somehow or other, allowed their infant children to get too close to the fireplace and get burned. One instance involved a rather upper crust white woman. The story was written with the utmost sympathy. Another concerned a black woman who had fallen upon the same misfortune. In so many words the writer, rather cruelly made it known that this occurred through carelessness on the part of the mother. I also read an article where a Native American kid was referred to as a "little heathen," but I can't remember the gist of the article. I also saw an article for Camel cigarettes where it was claimed that they "improved the digestion."

> Decades ago, when my paternal grandfather was alive, he was given a special treatment to help alleviate his asthma. What was it, you ask? He was advised to start smoking a pipe. Duh!

I also got hooked on the comic strip, *Alley Oop*, but I promise that I did get work done while I was working on this project. It was also featured in our local paper and I received a letter from one of our state representatives commending me for the index which was bound and is still available for use in the Genealogy Room.

I can't say that I am as much into genealogy as I was before I worked in the Genealogy Room. That's not the fault of the room, my time there, or any specific person, it's just that when you spend 16–20 hours a week around a particular subject, it sort of cools your enthusiasm. One thing that I never grow tired of, however, is the stories that people would tell and I got a lot of really great ones from the people who came into the Genealogy Room. One guy came in and told all of us that a close ancestor of his was arrested for killing someone with a cue ball. The guy's story was so outlandish that we had to ask him to repeat himself and at that prompting he stood up in the middle of the room and acted it out like he was on stage at the Globe Theatre. Apparently Grandpa got into it with another guy over who had the table next and in the altercation picked the cue ball up off the table and beaned the guy in the forehead with it, killing him instantly. Then he left the bar, the town and the state only to settle down in North Carolina and start a family which would lead to our performer coming to join us in the library that day.

Things Never to Say to a Librarian

1. (When asking a reference question) "I'm about to make you work for a living."
2. (When approaching the reference desk) "Wake up!"
3. "I wish I had your job. You get to read all day."
4. "You know I pay your salary." (Please know that we realize this and appreciate it, but you don't need to remind us of it daily.)
5. "Forget it. I'll just check Google."
6. "You're too sexy to be a librarian."

8

The Brotherhood/Sisterhood of the Book

For over fifteen years I can safely say that the local public library became my home away from home. Not only was I at work for just as long as I was at home (no surprise there; a lot of jobs are like that), but I became familiar with the staff there. For the great majority of that time, among the professional and paraprofessional librarians, there was no turnover. Sure, people came and went among the part timers, but the core group remained the same. The same positions were held by the same people and the departments functioned a particular way. Me, I got to work at roughly the same time every day, did roughly the same thing, went on break with the same people, and went to lunch at the same time at my parents' house where we watched the same soap operas together. Every Thursday I closed, so I did a split, and one Saturday out of every three I worked so I got that Friday off. I know this sounds incredibly boring, but as I look back on it, it was really comfortable and I look on those years fondly.

I would like to write a little bit about everyone I've ever worked with, but space limits that, and, since this book is supposed to be about library humor I want to include something about one person. Remember Queenie? I mentioned her earlier. That's not her real name but was a nickname I gave her, and those people who have worked with the both of us will know who I'm talking about. The reason that I'm including a section on her is that, as frustrating as she could be on occasion, I deeply miss working with her. Many is the time that I came to work perhaps tired, fed up or otherwise out of sorts. All I had to do was hunt up Queenie. Sometimes she would have some sort of silly story or opinion, or she would go off on some sort of funny rant. Sometimes we would even have a semi-

8. The Brotherhood/Sisterhood of the Book

serious disagreement, but regardless, it improved my mood more times than I could count.

Queenie worked in circulation, or lending (the terminology is different depending on the library) but her reach went way farther than that. She was active with our friends group as well as active in the community, and knew probably one out of every three people who came in the door on any given day, and if she didn't know you and you were a repeat customer, she would. There were two things that made Queenie who she was. One was that she was very particular, and two, despite her quirks she was a very big hearted person and the fact that she cared for people was obvious. I called her my fourth mother, since the care for me was definitely there, but growing up in a family full of women there were a couple of people ahead of her.

Queenie was very meticulous and everything around her had to be just so. My favorite example was how the books were filed when they were checked in and placed behind the circulation desk. The books were placed on the carts, not by Dewey number—which is how pretty much every other library does it—or maybe subject or category, but were arranged by height on the cart. Many is the time when I was feeling like a fight I would point out the fact that whoever had to shelve these books had to put them on another cart and arrange them all over again. We had some epic battles over this particular subject, but she was steadfast and that was the way the books were arranged for as long as she was over the circulation department. I also enjoyed sneaking over to circulation and putting a small book with the big ones or vice versa.

This wasn't the only quirk Queenie had in the running and the arrangement of the circulation department. When she would put a book under the scanner, if it didn't immediately register the barcode, she would whack the scanner with the book as if that would make it register any quicker. Also, in her closing routine—which took a long time and most of the time we would have to leave her in an empty building at night—she had to clean the dust out from inside the computer keyboards. This involved her banging the keyboards on the circulation desk so that any debris would fall out and could be swept into the trash can. On those rare occasions when she did leave with the rest of us, she would always stop by a sign that was right outside the main entrance and said "No Parking." It wasn't built into the concrete, it was on a stand, and she would rotate it one way and then back the other way to its original position.

My favorite Queenie story occurred one morning when she came to work complaining about a sore arm. When some of our co-workers and I asked her about her malady, she admitted that that morning she was running a little late. She was on her way out and noticed a wrinkle on the sleeve of her sweater. Ever

November 2004

Here in my
library I sit,
Amid rare volumes
richly bound,
A mine of cleverness
and wit,
From authors
Everywhere
Renowned.
-Quincy Kilby

Jon Farlow & Marsha Haithcock
Asheboro Public Library
Donna Miller
Friends of the Randolph Public Library

This picture is from a promotional calendar that the library had printed up. It shows a genuinely unique method that we used to shelve books.

particular, she stopped to iron out the wrinkle when the phone rang and she tried to iron it out holding the receiver under her chin. She was trying to remove the wrinkle, with a hot iron mind you, while she was wearing the sweater. We all had a good laugh over this and I brought it up for years afterward. The thing is, Queenie laughed too, which is what made it all the funnier, and she loved to laugh. She had a wild, manic cackle that really showed her love for anything funny.

Queenie was a little woman, probably five feet tall at the most, and I think she shrunk in the time I worked with her, but she was small in stature only. She could be a force of nature when she wanted to be. There used to be a homeless man named Buck who would hang around the courthouse, the library and that general area. Buck had a family and a place to go but his family would drop him off downtown so he could panhandle and otherwise harass people. One day he was sitting in a chair beside the library's main entrance begging people who entered and exited the place for money. The thing about Buck was that he was big and loud but he was harmless. Still, if someone didn't know him he could bully them into giving him money. Someone came in that morning after running the gauntlet with Buck and let Queenie know that somebody was panhandling in the lobby. She knew exactly who it was and marched down the stairs to confront Buck. She almost came up to his chest, when he was standing up, but he was sitting down and she was able to get in his face and told him to leave.

"Stop in the name of the Lord," Buck said.

"Get out in the name of me!" was Queenie's comeback as she yanked the chair out from behind him before he was standing up all the way and carried it back upstairs.

> As I said before, Buck would frequent the courthouse as well as the library, and one of the clerk of court offices was in the basement and had windows that were at ground level. One of these windows was in clear view of where Buck liked to answer the call of nature. From what I've heard through the grapevine, a couple of times one of the women who worked there would look up and through the window just in time to see a huge black man peeing mere inches away. One Halloween the ladies in the office decided to have a Buck party. They came to work dressed like Buck wearing overalls and flannel shirts with plenty of padding underneath. Along with refreshments they had lemonade punch, due to the urine-like yellow color.

One of my duties when I was at the library was as AV librarian. That is, I purchased and maintained things such as CDs, audiobooks, videos, DVDs and the like. One afternoon one of our video cases came in but the video in it had no markings. No stickers, no stamps no nothing. It could have been a personal tape but we weren't sure, so whoever noticed it when it was checked in brought it to me. I popped the video in my office's VCR and hit play. It took me just a couple of seconds to register what I was seeing, then it clicked that I was watching a porno. I turned it off after awhile and then called the patron's number that we had on record. I spoke to his wife and told her about the video and specifically what was on that video. She didn't sound surprised and I told her to pass on the message to her husband that he needed to come get his video and bring ours back. I told Queenie about the situation and we agreed that one of us was going to have to have a talk with the guy when he came in regarding responsible usage of library materials. I laugh about this now but it really could have been a lot worse than it was. The case that was sent back with the porn in it was for a movie called *Four Little Girls*. It's about the bombing of the 16th Street Baptist Church on September 15, 1963, that killed four little girls who were at the church for Sunday School. A child could have very easily viewed this video if the circulation department had failed to notice that it might not have been our video in the case. I wasn't there when the guy came back to get his video so he had to deal with Queenie. I heard that it wasn't pretty. She really ripped him a new one!

For awhile Queenie was an avid runner. She ran several miles a day religiously, rain or shine, although she was always concerned that someone would see her in sweats and a toboggan with no makeup. Sunday mornings were her mornings to walk at the city cemetery. One morning she was there and as she came around a bend she heard somebody yell, "Hey!" She looked over and saw a man lying on his back on the grass. His pants where open and partially down and his genitals were exposed. When he saw Queenie was looking, he pointed to his pecker with one hand. Queenie said she ran and some of the other walkers went back to look for him but he had already gone. I always liked to pick on Queenie about that incident, saying that if she would have been in church worshipping the Lord like she should have been she would not have been subject to such a spectacle.

I've said a lot about Queenie's humorous quirks, but to get a feel for the person she was, you have to understand how big-hearted and charitable a person she was. She was involved in a great many charities and made it a point to help people whenever she could, sparing no expense. I myself have been on the receiving end of her charitable side, as one year for Valentine's Day, she gave my wife and me a gift certificate for a really expensive restaurant. This was a gift that was greatly enjoyed and appreciated. It was a gift that she did not have to give, nor was it expected. There were two boys who lived beside the library. One was your stereotypical delinquent. The other was an intelligent, industrious young man who made good grades and had potential, but was still in danger of going down the same path as his brother. Queenie took a definite interest in the second kid to the point that he would bring her his report card so that she could make a big deal over his grades. I know she paid for his school supplies because this was not something that was being done at home, and she even bought him a set of dressy clothes because he was invited to a school program (because of his good academic performance) that required he be dressed up.

Before I left our county library system I spent a couple of years at one of our branches. In the months leading up to my departure, Queenie became quite ill with what was later revealed as cancer. The last time I talked to her was on the phone. I had been up for a promotion and it was pretty well known that I had my heart set on it. When I didn't get it she called to make sure I was okay, which was her way to the very end. We were all worried about her but she was worried about me over something as insignificant as being passed over for a job. A little disappointment is nothing compared to cancer. Not long after I started the job at our branch—not the job I wanted but a good experience nevertheless—we all received a systemwide e-mail that Queenie had passed away. It was difficult news to swal-

8. The Brotherhood/Sisterhood of the Book

low. Not long after that I had a dream that I was leaving the main library and as I headed across the parking lot I looked back and saw her silhouette in one of the large windows over the main entrance. I don't know if dreams always have a special meaning, but I guess Queenie was telling me goodbye, or maybe it was saying that she was and always will be part of that library. She's never left.

One of the best things about working with people that you know really well is that you can play practical jokes, and there were several in my time at my hometown library. The first one that I can remember was when I left an old classic on Queenie's desk, the old fake peanut brittle can with the snakes that popped out when you pulled off the lid. I didn't think that it would work. I mean nobody ever falls for that old joke, do they? I know one person that did. I bid Queenie good morning as she came in and watched her as she disappeared into her cubicle. In a couple of minutes the two snakes shot up above the cubicle wall and then disappeared behind it. This was followed by a wild cackle of laughter.

A co-worker got Queenie good one night when a visiting storyteller had left the rabbit that he used in his act in the co-worker's care. The co-worker got it out and smuggled the rabbit into circulation where she left it on a bottom shelf. This was a very well-trained, very calm rabbit, because it just sat there where she put it. That is, until Queenie turned around, saw it and screamed, which made the poor creature bolt down through the offices shooting little round pellets out of its butt as it went. Queenie gave chase all the time screaming, "Don't Poopie! Don't Poopie!" which made the rabbit poopie more and it laid a trail of little black beads as it zig zagged in and out of each cubicle.

There was another time when I put a rubber snake in the book drop. One of the ladies at circulation emptied the drop but didn't notice it until she got the full container back up to the lending desk and reached in to start pulling out books. I wasn't there when she found the snake but, from what I understand, she was quite startled, and when I asked her about it she accused me of making her curse. She took the snake away from me and put it in somebody's office. Then it sort of made the rounds throughout the building, and the last time I saw it the director had confiscated it and was placing it in his desk drawer. I also brought a remote control fart machine that made the rounds before somebody found it under a book cart in her office and thought it was some sort of bomb. Eventually, like the snake, it was confiscated by somebody or other and it was awhile before I saw it again.

I told a co-worker of mine at the branch library where I worked for awhile about the "snake in the book drop" joke and he started telling me about all the strange items that he, or librarians he had talked to, had found in book drops. Most of the time these items were some type of refuse because, Lord knows, a library book drop sure looks a lot like a garbage can. Librarians have also found mail due to the fact that somebody mistook the book drop for a mailbox. There have also been things of a more disgusting nature, such as dirty diapers or food. The librarian telling me this said the strangest thing he ever found in a book drop was a pumpkin flavored latte that had splashed all over the books and other materials in the box when it was dropped in.

My favorite practical joke was pulled by a co-worker and I on another co-worker while she was away on vacation. What we did was sneak into her cubicle and empty out her desk drawers. Then we lined them with tin foil and filled all of them to the rim with jelly beans. Then there was the long wait until she came back from vacation. When she did, and discovered our improvement to her office, her reaction was what made the joke worthwhile. She told us later that she really loved what we had done because, not only did she love jelly beans, but also we had brought a smile to her face. Apparently, while she was on vacation, her roommate had passed away and she had still been grieving when she came back to work. When she had seen all of her desk drawers full of jelly beans, that had been the first time she had smiled since the tragedy. That was the best joke that I've ever played on anybody and what made it worthwhile was bringing a smile to someone's face.

Christmas was always an interesting time at the library. Throughout the staff we had varying degrees of Christmas spirit from manic, Queenie, to I'm a proud Scrooge I don't want to hear it, Mr. Benz. When I first got to the library Christmas carols were piped in over the PA system. The following year the Scrooges won an important victory and the practice was ended. We still had our yearly Christmas party, however, with delicious food, music and, when my talent for acting silly became apparent, I started providing the entertainment. My dog and pony show, so to speak, first consisted of stories that I had written including the staff as characters. I can't remember all of them but one was from the point of view of the library Christmas tree and another was the library *Christmas Carol* with, you guessed it, Benz as Scrooge. One of the running jokes during my entertainment section of the program was that I tried to get Santa Claus every year but each time I wasn't able to get the genuine article because he and his impersonators were busy that time of the year. One year I had one of our regulars who had a flair for the dramatic come in and pretend to be a homeless person I had paid to be Santa Claus. He came in unshaven wearing a dirty Santa hat with an old terry cloth bathrobe open to expose a dirty t-shirt and matching warm-up pants. He had a trash bag slung over his shoulder and proceeded to hand out presents which included strands of dental floss, used batteries and other such valuable prizes. Another year I had the Easter Bunny come in and start handing out candy canes.

8. The Brotherhood/Sisterhood of the Book

The joke behind her appearance was that she was cheap this time of the year when Santa Claus was unavailable. In reality the Easter Bunny was a co-worker who came hopping in with bunny ears and a cotton tail attached to the seat of her pants and started handing out candy. At least that was the plan. After she had done that, she sat down on a co-worker's lap and asked him what he wanted for Christmas. That was something I did not anticipate and, although I thought almost everybody present thought it was pretty funny, that was the last Christmas party. I think someone complained and I never knew what to think of that or what part I played in it, but I enjoyed it while it lasted.

During the Christmas we were at the temporary facility, one of the local home school associations had a contest where the students made gingerbread houses. The top three were given ribbons and displayed at the library. One day while the houses were on display, one of the children's librarians saw a man hanging around the houses. This guy did not look like your average patron who would hang around the children's room, nor one who would have any interest in gingerbread houses. In fact the librarian said he looked homeless. After he had been hanging around for almost 45 minutes to an hour the librarian went to check on what he was doing. When she got around to the far side of the gingerbread houses, she found that they had been stripped bare, every piece of peppermint, every gumdrop, every string of icing was missing. She looked up at the patron who had stuffed his hands in the pockets of his old army fatigue jacket and did his best to appear casual. His cheeks were bulging out like a chipmunk's, giving her a definite clue as to the location of the missing candy.

"Sir, I wouldn't eat those," the librarian told him as he wiped some drool from his lip. "They've been lacquered." The librarian said that the guy seemed to think about the situation, then he swallowed hard and left.

Another story I always think of when I hear the last one, the two of which inspired a short story, involved another home school project. One group did a project on ancient Egypt and displayed it in the children's room. There were models of pyramids, translations of hieroglyphics and the like plus one ambitious student had mummified a rat. He had reportedly used the exact techniques the Egyptians used to mummify the rodent and displayed him in a large flat dish. After a couple of days the rat started stinking. The children's room staff stood it for as long as they could and then the head of the room called the mother and asked that she come pick it up. The lady was very obliging and promised to come by and get it that day. She arrived within a few hours and again was friendly and ready to help. She took the rat, dropped it into her large mom sized pocketbook along with the dish, smiled, bid the librarians goodbye and left. I could always see the woman stopping at a supermarket or department store and having to go through her pocketbook at the counter looking for her checkbook. I visualized her pulling the rat out and plopping it onto the counter with her car keys, Kleenex and all the other flotsam that moms carry with them.

    I sat down with a former co-worker of mine and we started talking about the unusual subject of patron nicknames. She describes librarians as "muppets" on display to the patrons. Because of this she says that it can be difficult when discussing certain situations or patrons without using nicknames for some of our more colorful patrons. She talks about this method as a way to talk about certain patrons without being too obvious, while simultaneously showing off their own senses of humor. For instance, there is a patron with a very long beard, who is vastly tall and rather gaunt. We called him "mountain man." After I left, the *Harry Potter* movies hit their stride at the box office and faded into pop culture immortality, so the staff began to note the resemblance of this patron to Albus Dumbledore, the headmaster of Hogwarts School of Witchcraft and Wizardry, so they refer to him as "Dumbledore." There's another patron who, when asked how he is, always answers, "I'm still looking down at the grass," so he is "Looking Down at the Grass Man." There is another vagrant-type who lives in the woods and drives a dirt bike everywhere and brings tiny bits of woodland debris in to be identified. My friend calls the man "The Wanderer" but another colleague named him "Dirt Bike Old Man" which apparently the staff likes better. Personally I like "The Wanderer," or maybe I would have named him "Easy Rider." One old randy rascal always comes in bringing with him an air of some serious illness and always wears a child's woven straw cowboy hat. He is quick to tell anyone who would listen, but mostly cute younger women, of his time in the Air Force, and his fondness for Frank Zappa. When the patron found out that my friend was a Zappa fan as well, the patron became somewhat of a pain and would hang around for hours wheezing and coughing in between his rants concerning the modern music scene and a school principal who had "labeled" him as a sex offender, for prowling school playgrounds. The staff called him "The Flying Cowboy." Once, he came in with a hat that looked for all the world like a hat that Huggy Bear, from the TV show *Starsky and Hutch* would have worn, being deep purple in color, covered in velvet, and rather pimpish. So, he was bumped up to "The Velvet Cowboy," after that. Two separate patrons apparently have a fascination with the Marvel Comics hero Wolverine, and so became "Yellow Wolverine" and "Purple Brown Suit Wolverine," respectively. Yellow Wolverine was shorter, slightly smelling of cigars and was gruff-looking, like a skid row version of the actual Wolverine. The other was not nearly as tall and he sported a purple goatee.

    An extremely obese man, with a penchant for wearing red t-shirts, became known as "The Killer Tomato," in reference to the B-movie *Attack of the Killer*

8. The Brotherhood/Sisterhood of the Book

Tomatoes. When he wore a green tee, he became "The Killer Green Tomato." I would have preferred "The Fried Green Tomato." His son, or his younger, slightly less obese companion was "Son of The Killer Tomato." A younger patron—frequently drunk, looking every bit like nothing but trouble, from his dog choker necklace, to his Axl Rose bandana and aviator sunglasses—became simply, "The Aviator." The last patron my friend mentioned is the "Lone Strummer," a local favorite, whose bizarre habit of pinching the female reference librarians, makes him entertaining for some, but extremely annoying to others.

The thing about my time at that library was that the patrons were almost as consistent as the staff. For years the same people came in at the same time of the same day of the week and looked up what looked like the same kinds of information. It would take too much time and space to mention them all, but my favorite provided so much entertainment that he inspired probably the most popular character in the books and stories I have written. The character's name is Slobber McAllister, so that's what I'll call the patron. Slobber would come in daily to get on the Internet and browse for things on cartoons, science fiction and old TV shows, among other things of which he had an almost encyclopedic knowledge. He rode a scooter and would come in, day or night, hot or cold, in a thick quilted coat and an expensive looking motorcycle helmet that covered his face with a flip up visor. If he was in a bad mood, or didn't feel particularly sociable, he would leave his helmet on while he was on the computer and just flip up the visor so he could see the monitor. A couple of times when Queenie caught him doing this, she would walk up behind him and rap sharply on the back of his helmet with her knuckles and tell him to take it off. He wasn't happy about it but he always complied.

When Slobber was in a good mood and talkative, that was when he really lent a lot of entertainment value to our day. One time he walked up to the reference desk and informed the librarian on duty that the doctor had given him something "to make him poop."

"I don't need to know that," the librarian was quick to say.

"So who else is here?" Slobber was one of Queenie's favorite targets when she got a mind to improve someone's life, whether they liked it or not. For a while she was onto him to improve his checkerboard smile and at her urging he made an appointment with a free dentist at the health department. There was a lot of work to do in Slobber's mouth and this caused him a great deal of discomfort while the lady dentist was working. Apparently he called her a few choice names and offended her to the point that she refused to do any more work on him. So the next time he came in, his checkerboard smile had devolved into a black-toothed grin. Queenie would also get onto him about his weight, as he was a rather rotund fellow, and one day he must have gotten tired of it because on the way out she brought up his waistline yet again. He stopped, turned to face her, and, taking his rather pendulous belly in both hands, shook it at her while saying, "Wobble. Wobble. Wobble."

My favorite Slobber story concerned his sister's dog. He lived in a trailer behind his sister and brother-in-law's house. One summer they went on vacation and left their small dog in the care of Slobber. I don't know the reason, but Slobber started feeding the dog biscuits and gravy instead of dog food, and the poor thing became constipated. Afraid of drawing the ire of his sister when she got back Slobber took the dog to the vet who suggested that he give the dog an enema, which he attempted when he got home, with a water hose. As expected, that didn't work out too well and Slobber, as well as the dog, ended up back at the vet where I hope he was told why it's a bad idea to give dogs enemas with water hoses. The doctor told him to buy some pumpkin pie filler and feed it to the dog, which did cure the dog's constipation, but not the trauma of having a water hose roughly crammed up your rectum. Eventually something happened to Slobber's scooter so he lost his transportation to the library. His brother said that he had never heard of motor oil and didn't know that he was supposed to put some into his engine periodically. After that he would call daily and ask cryptic questions regarding cartoons and obscure Japanese monster movies, remaining a colorful patron even though he wasn't there in person.

Every time I talk about wild patrons I can't help but think of Slobber as well as one month when we seemed inundated with nut jobs, and he was not one of them. I mentioned this spell earlier when I talked about the man who came into the Genealogy Room to steal purses and saw fit to sign in and use his real information. I can't remember the month or the season but in a single month we had to ban four patrons within thirty days. The first one was the guy from the Genealogy Room. The second was a young man who set about going through our entire collection and drawing dirty pictures and writing obscene statements on the pages. I don't know how long he was at it, but it wasn't long before I left the library that we were still finding them. The next culprit was a man who would go out and pray in our parking lot. He would go to the little driveway where the Extension Department parked their vans, get on his knees and press his forehead to the pavement in a decidedly Islamic fashion. When he was questioned about it, he did admit to the librarian who asked him, that he was Muslim. But someone did a little research and found out that, if he was Muslim, he was not facing Mecca, which is the custom. That would have been strange, but not enough to get him thrown out. What did that was that he proceeded to tear the covers off several paperbacks. The third incident involved a local character that caused several stirs around town, not just at the library. This lady had some sort of obsession with Elvis and believed that he was alive. One day in the library as she was checking out, she leaned over the desk and confided in the women there, "There is a rumor around town that I am having an affair with Elvis," she whispered. "Well I don't even know the f*****g man." A friend of my nephew went to church with the woman, and said that she would come to the service and as the choir was singing the opening hymn she would get up, leave and go grocery shopping. Then, as the minister was wrapping up his sermon she would return, her arms loaded with grocery bags and go back to her pew until the service was over. What got her banned from the library was that she came in to check out some materials and couldn't because she had an outstanding balance on her card and it was beyond the limit to let her check out anything else. She argued with a couple of the librarians for a few minutes and then stomped out, but before she left she walked up behind one of the other librarians, who was about to go through the door to administration, and kicked her in the seat of the pants, which resulted in this librarian having back problems from then on.

Did the expulsion of these four unruly patrons solve our nutty patron problem? No. Remember, nutty patrons are like the hydra from Greek mythology. You get rid of one and two will grow in their place.

9

Oh, Christmas Tree

I mentioned in the last chapter that for a few years I was in charge of the entertainment at the library's Christmas party. One of the things I would do would be to write a Christmas story using the staff as characters. The first one that I wrote used the library Christmas tree as a main character and I think that it went over really well. I have included this story here. It's meant to be read aloud as opposed to being read, and it should be read in a very flamboyant lisp sort of like Truman Capote. It was featured in the December 2004 edition of our library newsletter.

Oh, Christmas Tree
A Story by Jonathan Farlow

EDITOR'S NOTE: The following is a work of fiction. Any resemblance to Christmas trees living or dead is entirely suspicious.

You just don't know what it's like to be a Christmas tree. It's not all glitz and glamour, I'll tell you that. Well maybe human beings would like to be yanked up from the exact spot of their birth only to stand in a mall parking lot for days, weeks until maybe, just maybe some toothless redneck or, oh even worse, some dad with mommy and the little brats in tow chooses them for some inane reason. They strap you to the SUV and take you home only to decorate you with the most degrading, tacky, homemade Christmas ornaments that little Buffy or Jo-Jo made at daycare with their own little Vienna sausage fingers. Of course the only time you get watered during those long tortuous weeks is when the family mutt wanders by. Then, just as the last of your needles is desperately hanging on to your limbs, you get yanked up again, stripped naked and tossed out onto the curb in front of God and everybody for Burney or Wade to shove you into a chipper shredder and that's that.

Of course it's different for artificial trees, you're probably saying right about now. I can give you my own personal testimony in that regard. I'm of the fake variety, a replica of a Bradford fir, nine feet, full majestic worthy of nothing less than total admiration by those whose presents are nurtured, protected beneath my boughs. For those of you who don't have a Funk and Wagnall's handy, total admiration does not include having your limbs wrenched from your trunk and stuffed into a box for eleven months out of the year. I had a friend whose owner is a bachelor, lived in a little two bedroom frame house on the other side of town. The guy was a slob to be quite frank and, according to my friend, as lazy as they come. After Christmas he would just leave my friend together and still decorated, slide him into the extra bedroom and then back out the next Christmas. Other than the beer bottle Christmas lights, he said that it wasn't a bad existence. Where is my place of display every holiday season? They set me up at the local library. Oh yes, I can hear you now. "Oh, but it's so peaceful at the library. Everybody in town gets to see you on display, oh I'll bet it's wonderful." Let me tell you.

I get dragged out of storage just before Thanksgiving by the same two guys every year, one getting on up there and the other is younger and pretty good looking if I may say so. They put me together and set me up and I've just gotten a chance to stretch my limbs before they show up. As soon as my backside is warm in it's stand those two old women launch themselves from around the front counter and descend on me like buzzards on a carcass.

"Oh it's crooked!" the blonde one shrieks.

"And Bill," the other one nags. "Look at the limbs." She takes out a ruler and looks through her bifocals. "This limb is one one-thousandth of an inch off. This just isn't going to cut it!" They banter around for awhile and after the men leave the women do over what they just did. Then they dust me off and spray me with pine scented spray, which is pretty insulting for a fir. They'll get the lights strung on me, all the time yak, yak, yak and finally leave me alone for the night. The next morning whoever the two old women asked, hired or threatened come in and decorate me. I do have to say these are the more pleasant moments of the yearly routine. Whatever the decoration, candy, bows, origami or magnolias made from balloons, I always look top notch. In fact, when everybody's gone I turn around so I can get a good look of myself in the window, and if it's late enough and there's nobody on the street I move stuff around to make sure that everything looks perfect.

I do have to do this on a nightly basis because when the holiday's over the doors open and the public comes in. You don't really expect anybody to leave anything alone do you? Kids take stuff off me, adults take stuff off me, staff takes stuff off me. There's the tall blonde guy who always seems to be in a bad mood at Christmas who, and I'm sure it's intentional, knocks decorations off of me and "accidentally" steps on them. One year this guy wearing a pith helmet walked up and started eating candy canes right off my branches. One of the ladies from the children's room informed him that they were treated, but it didn't seem to matter. He just kept on eating until he got full and then the Boy Scouts brought more. And another thing: you remember what I said about the family dog watering the Christmas tree? It's not just dogs who do that, but that's all I'm saying about that.

I guess all in all it's a good existence, could be worse I guess. At least there's no chipper shredder. At least there wasn't. I was standing there Friday in all my majestic glory. The old women were pulling and poking and moving and primping. The dark headed one was wetting me down with that infernal pine scented spray when she had the gall, the all out nerve to say, "This tree has been looking ratty, we sure need a new one." Of course her little buddy agreed.

"Oh yeah," she scrunched her nose up like she smelled something. "We ought to throw this thing away and get a new one next year."

"Yeah, let's talk that over with Richard." Can you believe it? All those years of standing here, all the Christmas cheer that I have brought to this library. The poking, the primping, that cramped box all off-season, the kids, the adults, the staff. That accursed spray and they think that they're going to throw me away and replace me with some twig. Let me tell you I simmered all weekend. Sunday morning I was standing there looking out the window seething when the dark headed one jogged by. I could hardly recognize her. She didn't have on her nice clothes. She didn't have on her, good Lord, makeup, but it was her and just seeing her ticked me off to the point that I just had to do something. I started my top swaying, then that got my middle going then I started moving my bottom until I was leaning to and fro. I just kept myself swaying until, finally, splat. I fell over and let me tell you I blew those little origami animals as far as the door. I wish I could have seen her face when she jogged by the next time and couldn't see me on the carpet, but I was face down on the carpet. I heard her gasp and curse under her breath when she came up the stairs and in what seemed like seconds the other one was there groaning and fussing. They got me stood up and got the decorations back on me, the ones that weren't flat, that is. Of course I fell over again after they left and they had to do the same thing Monday morning and they will tomorrow and the next day. If they're going to put me out to pasture they're going to work for it, I'm telling you.

Well I don't guess you've enjoyed my story. I guess if you want an uplifting tale you might want to check somewhere else. I'm sure that if you have any scruples at all, and I'd like to think that there are still one or two people that do, you're

9. Oh, Christmas Tree

probably asking what can I do to sort of correct all this. One thing that does come to mind is that this Christmas while you're opening dozens of really nice presents or sitting down to a table piled high with mouthwatering food, take a minute to remember those of us who can't. Oh look, here come those ladies again. They've brought those guys with them to re-decorate me and shove me back in the box. If I lean just right I'll take them down with me this time.

10

Rats

In a previous chapter I mentioned how the regular library patron whom I called "Slobber" inspired a character in several short stories and a couple of novels that I've written. Of course his name, or his nickname for that matter, wasn't Slobber, but I've gone to great lengths in this book to keep the real names of people a secret to avoid embarrassing anybody, or any potential lawsuits. No, Slobber McAllister was the name that I gave the character because I wanted him to be sort of the ultimate social misfit. Someone with no graces in that regard and who could essentially be my comic relief as the patron was so good in doing. I thought that the nickname Slobber would be prime for a character like that and one that a person of this type would go by. McAllister was simply the name of a street near the library and I thought it flowed well with Slobber. In a way Slobber is sort of like my Holden Caulfield. People who have read my stuff ask about him the most and he seems to be the character that people remember. He has been in more of my writing than any other character. I am including this short story that features him. Remember he is a great deal like the real person.

Rats

... was the first thing out of Michael Frye's mouth the first second, of the first minute, of the first hour of the first day of his fourth summer vacation. The day before at exactly 2:45–2:47 by his watch—the final school bell shot him as well as every other student at Philip L. Shore Elementary School out the front doors and into the sunshine like a blessed cannon. For Michael it was an important vacation. He had just finished the fourth grade. He was nine years old. This would be the summer that his mother really cut him loose. He had the ten acre wood behind his

10. Rats

parents' house to explore, a brand new Evel Knievel bicycle, two family trips and exactly two months twenty-one days eight hours and fifteen minutes to do it in.

He had set his Washington Redskins alarm clock for six even though that was a good hour before his mother would wake him up on a school day, but summer vacation started the minute you woke up on that first day and time was marching on. The clock was one of the old fashioned type with the duel bells on top and the hammer in between that would bang against them both when the appropriate time came around. He had gotten it for Christmas and had never really figured out how it worked. He had never set it before that first day, however, and he stared in disgust as the hour hand slowly crept past eight.

He bounded out of bed and dressed in his favorite pair of jeans and tennis shoes, the ones with the holes, and the KISS t-shirt that he wasn't allowed to wear to school. He headed toward the door stopping only to look in on his hamster Roscoe, study a model of a viper from Battlestar Galactica that he was working on, and give a good swift kick to his book bag that had been tossed in a corner when he had gotten home from school the day before. Then he threw open the door and rushed out ready to tackle the first day of his vacation and tripped over a large wood and wire cage that was sitting in the hallway. He flipped over onto his seat and crab walked back in horror, not from the loud cooing and rustling that issued forth from the cage but from the strange man in the pin striped suit and bow tie who bent down over him.

"Oh my gracious!" the stranger said and, offering no more than a glance to Michael, picked up the cage, held it just an inch, if that much, from his own face and started making kissie noises through the fine wire mesh that concealed the contents. "Ow didm' get scared. Didm' bump their little head." Michael's mom, Anne, who stood on the other side of the man, mirrored her son's expression but did her best to swallow it.

"I'm sorry he didn't see the bird's cage."

"Well." The stranger lowered the cage to his side by the handle and held it like a suitcase. He flashed them both a rather strained looking smile underneath a pencil thin mustache. "Maybe I shouldn't be setting my things in front of people's doors." The look on Anne's face relaxed a little and she gestured to her son who was just then getting to his feet.

"This is my..."

"Hello," the stranger said, turning away from them and cutting off Anne with the wave of a hand over his shoulder. Then he sort of floated down the hall and disappeared into the extra bedroom where Anne kept her sewing machine.

Michael didn't ask the $25,000 question until he was sitting down at the table with Captain Crunch and the Quik Rabbit.

"Who is that?"

"His name is Harold," answered his mother from the sink where she was washing dishes. "He's renting a room from us for the furniture market in High Point."

"Why didn't anyone tell me that we were going to have strange people staying in our house?"

"Michael I did tell you just after we arranged it. It was right before Easter, you remember?" She turned to face her son whose blank expression told her the negative.

"You're just like your father. He forgot too. I tried to call him at the station but he was out. I hope he gets the message." The remainder of breakfast was silent save the wet crunch of Michael's cereal. Then he dropped his bowl, spoon and glass into the sink.

"What's Harold's last name?"

"I think that is his last name." Anne toweled off her hands and poured herself another cup of coffee. "Then again maybe not. I'm not sure he just said Harold. He paid in cash so I really have no way of knowing. He works for Langstrom Industries, some big furniture company out of Savannah. That's all I know."

"He's a little weird isn't he?"

"Michael, saying that man is a little weird," Anne said as she sat down at the table and opened her newspaper with a flip, "is like saying that your father is a little overweight."

As Michael was heading outdoors, his overweight father was sprinting around a dilapidated single-wide while simultaneously vaulting over the engine block of a 67 Mustang and spraying mace over his right shoulder in a feeble attempt to slow the pursuit of a 90 pound pit bull named LeAnn. The trailer, the engine block and LeAnn belonged to one Jay Vern Jones to whom Officer Grady Frye, along with his partner Leon Schaler, were trying to serve a warrant for his arrest when they were somewhat distracted by the sight of LeAnn coming at them from the backyard dragging a rather large chain. Jones had been arrested and placed on probation for stealing a neighbor's self-propelled push mower and attempting to ride it up Old Rail Yard Road to the Pantry to buy beer. He violated the probation when he brought a urine sample to a mandatory drug test and turned up pregnant.

While Grady and Leon were at his trailer to serve the warrant for missing his court date, Jay Vern was hiding in an old deer stand two miles back in the woods and listening to LeAnn barking as she cornered the two policemen on top of their squad car until animal control could arrive.

10. Rats

Anne had said that it was okay for Michael to go outside and officially begin his summer vacation with the agreement that he stay close.

"We've got some other people coming that should be getting here any minute and they may have some stuff that they need help bringing in." With that statement Michael's mother seriously put a cramp in his plans. He had places to go and things to see, a lot of ground to cover. All of this, three months and counting and now he had to stay in the yard and waste his precious time.

The grass was still wet as he stomped down across the yard and drops of dew shone in the sunlight of the new day like diamonds. He went around back of the outbuilding to the shelter where his dad kept fire wood and crouching down looked into a hole in the red dirt up against one shelter wall. It was there that he had seen two big rats a couple of weeks before. He had just stood and watched them that first time, half on his bicycle, transfixed as they sniffed around the woodpile and then disappeared down the hole. As he stood this morning there was no sign of them and walking over to the opposite wall he retrieved his BB gun off the top of the woodpile. His dad would've skinned him if he knew that he had left his gun out there, but he had kicked himself that he hadn't had it that first day, so he left it down there just in case.

He squatted down and sighted the hole. He squeezed the trigger and watched the tiny metal ball rocket down the hole, bouncing off the dirt and wood, spiraling down the tunnel where through a great feat of marksmanship it would kill both rats, two with one shot. In reality he never squeezed the trigger nor had he cocked the gun, but in his mind he rehearsed for the day that he would catch one or both in the open and that would be all she wrote.

He put his gun back on the woodpile and laid a wide piece of bark on top of it so his Dad wouldn't find it. He then pulled the sheet off his new bicycle, which was padlocked to one of the shelter's wooden supports, and wiped it off. Then he felt the tires to make sure they had air and oiled the chain again before he undid the lock with the key that he kept around his neck. He saddled up and headed around the shelter towards the driveway where he had planned on practicing wheelies, when he heard a strange noise coming from down the driveway toward the road. It was sort of a high pitched hum like the toy planes that they flew at the beach, but it was louder and it was getting closer real quick. His mother stepped out onto the porch and called him just as a big van flew up the hill and into the yard where the rest of the cars were parked and stopped next to Harold's brick colored Saab. Michael hadn't noticed him as they whipped by because he had been concealed in the vapor trail of dust left by the van, but a guy on a scooter stopped right behind them and switching off the motor started taking off what to Michael looked like an old army helmet.

Michael went back around to the shelter, dusted off his bicycle, covered it back up, chained it back to the support and as he rushed toward the house his mother was already calling him again. When he got there Harold was out on the porch and the two ladies had gotten out of the van. One of the women was thin and wore a bright yellow moo-moo that sort of flapped as she walked, matching sandals and a floppy white hat with daisies growing off the brim. She practically pranced up to the porch steps while the other woman slid open the van's side door and started pulling packages and boxes out. Anne directed her son with a snap and a point to help carry stuff and as he walked up behind the second woman he saw that she was no taller or no wider than he was. She smiled at him as he took a small purple makeup case from her and then turned back, her dangly earrings slapping the side of her neck.

He dropped the case onto one of the twin beds in the room between Harold's and his own and ran back down like a kid who had dashed to the bathroom during a movie. No one else was lifting a finger. Harold was still standing on the porch and the skinny woman was standing at the bottom of the stairs like a native paying tribute to the king of the tribe.

"My name is Jennifer Wilcox," she was saying, "and this is my sister Dottie." She gestured to the little woman as she passed by her and headed toward the van again. She was wearing a long denim skirt and that, as well as her sister's height, by contrast made her seem even smaller.

"Yes, hello." Harold's voice took on the same condescending tone that it had upstairs. "We spoke on the phone. Is this the artist that you've been raving to my company about?"

"Oh yes, this is Ambrose." She took the man by the arm and led him from where he stood by his scooter to the steps.

"Hello," Harold spoke in that same strained sounding voice. The other man just stood by Jennifer Wilcox and nodded his head. He looked like he hadn't had a shave in a week or two and his salt and pepper hair was slicked down to his head from where he had been wearing the helmet which he carried in one hand. With the other he held a half-empty trash bag against a substantial gut. He didn't speak for a few seconds and when he did, no one acted like they heard him.

"My name's Slobber. I like to be called Slobber." No one acknowledged the man save Michael who thought that Slobber was a weird name but it did fit the stranger better than Ambrose, which sounded more at home on Harold who now floated down off the stairs to look at the artist a little closer.

"So this is our great find. Your diamond in the rough."

"Oh yes. He's done one piece that we're particularly proud of. It's an oaken headboard with a motif that's based on a Japanese myth."

"Hmmm," said Harold, his interest piqued.

"It's Godzilla," said Slobber, but the only one who seemed to hear him was Michael.

"And Ambrose has informed us that the legend is circa 56 AD."

"That's 1956." Again, no one seemed to pay attention to Slobber except for Michael who was so engrossed in the conversation that he stood there beside the van holding a Pepsi box full of paperwork until his Mother slapped him on the back of the head and got him moving toward the house.

Within the hour everyone was gone and the house was just as it had been before they got there, save Ambrose/Slobber's trash bag thrown into the corner of Michael's room along with a folded up army cot since he was, as Anne had bluntly informed her son, sleeping in Michael's room. Michael slumped around the house muttering, "Damn, damn, damn, damn," under his breath, which was the only cuss word that he really knew. His spirits did lift, however, when he stalked to the back door, looked out through the screen and realized that he was free to resume his summer vacation.

This time he hadn't even gotten the cover off his bicycle when his mother's shrill voice echoed yet again down over the backyard.

"I need to go get a haircut and run by the grocery store so don't go anywhere."

A toy pistol that shot plastic BBs helped to appease Michael at the grocery store and lunch at Ray's Burgers made him down right giddy by the time that he and Anne got back home. After Michael helped his mother bring in groceries, most of the day was lost but he still had enough time to ride down to the creek before his dad got home. He took his real BB gun slung across his back and the toy one stuck in the band of his jeans in case he saw a possum, raccoon or mink that his dad said messed around down by the water. When he stopped by the shelter to get his gun and bicycle, he checked to see if he saw anything of the rats. They were gone leaving neither turd nor track as a sign of their being there.

He was watching a crawdad crawl under a rock with a chewed piece of bubble gum when the voice that he had learned to dread like a booster shot again called him, this time for dinner. When he got in, stopping to clean, cover and chain his bicycle, everyone, including the houseguests, were sitting around the table like a strange cross of the Addams family and the Culhanes of Cornfield County from *Hee Haw*. His dad was home and they said hey with a quick glance. He, Anne, Harold and the Wilcox sisters were sitting around the table in the alcove off the kitchen and Michael was directed to sit on a stool at the bar where he ate his breakfast, with Slobber.

"I hope everything's okay?" Anne asked after awhile. Everyone nodded the affirmative except for Slobber who shoveled a large mound of mashed potatoes into his mouth, and Harold, who was busy separating the peas from his stew with his butter knife.

"Well it's not what I'm used to but it'll have to do," he said stabbing a carrot and slipping it into his mouth as if it were covered with quills.

"I think it's very good Anne," said Jennifer as she spooned some of each onto her plate. Anne started to respond but Harold broke in while the words were still dancing up her tongue.

"I do trust that the pieces that are arriving tomorrow are better than the ones that we viewed this afternoon. Those were adequate, but hardly exemplary, and the nightstand on crab's legs, although it did draw some praise from a couple of the younger viewers, did not impress the important people."

"Mie Mumph thut uh Muffa Mun," Slobber was speaking, but a mouthful of potatoes made his words impossible to understand, not that anyone was listening except Michael, who wiped off a piece of chewed up meat which had flown from Slobber's mouth and landed on his cheek.

"Um, well the best pieces are on the truck and I do apologize for it not being here yet. Our brother's rather bad with directions." Jennifer was grasping for words while Dottie simply sat and looked down into a cleaned plate, smiling at the conversation going on around the table.

"He'd best get here tomorrow. Langstrom Industries did not put money into this project to be led around by the nose. We put in the cash and we want to see the goods, and choice merchandise. We're particularly hoping that this Japanese headboard will make the collection because so far nothing else has." Jennifer put out her hands as if she were afraid he would hit her and did her best to explain.

"I assure you that the goods will be here and they will exceed your expectations. The headboard that I spoke of alone will..."

"That's Godzilla on it though," Slobber had finished what had been on his plate and had come over to the table to get a refill.

"Excuse me, Miss Wilcox," Harold held up his hand and then pointed a long finger at Slobber who looked at it like it was dessert to go with his stew and potatoes. "Would you please be quiet and leave the talking to those of us who know what they're talking about. Yes, thank you." Slobber simply went back to his stool like he didn't understand what was just said to him or didn't care. Harold said a few more choice words and went upstairs.

While Jennifer and Dottie were helping Anne clear the table and do the dishes, Michael sat on his father's lap while they watched *The Dukes of Hazzard* as they always did on Friday nights. Slobber sat on the couch and watched with them, not saying a word the entire time. At bedtime Michael got into his pajamas and went into the bathroom to brush his teeth. When he got back Slobber was standing over his desk looking at the partially assembled Viper model.

"This gonna be a Viper? Like they got on *Battlestar Galactica*?"

"Uh yeah." Just the fact that a grown up was taking an interest in something he was doing made Michael ease up just a little bit towards his new roommate.

"Well that's cool. I never miss *Galactica*."

"Yeah?"

"Yeah, you heard they getting sued, though didn't you?"

"No, What about?"

"That guy that did *Star Wars* is suing 'em cause its looks too much like *Star Wars*."

"I guess they do, but I like 'em both."

"Yeah man." Slobber turned around and started unfolding the cot. For some reason Michael wanted to keep the conversation going. They discussed *Galactica* some more, then Ultraman and comic books. Slobber liked Spiderman, while Michael had always been a DC fan and favored Batman and he never missed a rerun of the old cheesy TV show. When they turned to Godzilla and Slobber started giving the merits of the first film as the best of the series and explaining the connection between the movies and the anxiety of the Japanese people toward atomic energy stemming from the dropping of the first atomic bomb on Hiroshima a little over ten years before the movie was released, Michael started to doze off. When he woke up about half an hour later, Slobber was still talking.

Michael was sitting at his desk in his pajamas the next morning working on his Viper model. The window was open and the old fan that Anne had rescued from his grandmother's yard sale was sitting just inside it, the metal blades sucking in the fresh, rain-smelling air from outside. His mother made him work on his model by the window because of the glue fumes. She didn't want him to get loopy.

He had just put a generous helping of glue on the last piece, getting a lot on his hands as well, when a big white bird streaked by him like a rocket and flew into the fan. Anne was coming up to her son's room that very second to see if he wanted any breakfast and found him frozen where he sat and covered with white, downy feathers which were also laying over the desk, the floor, and lingering in the air around him.

"What in God's name!" she shrieked as she ran to him and started frantically plucking feathers out of his hair.

"Was that a bird?" As Michael spoke a feather flew out of his mouth.

"Oh no! Did it kill it? We have got to get that bird back!" Anne went to the window and looked down into the yard just as their neighbor's black lab scooped the still quivering bird up into its mouth and trotted triumphantly back towards home. "It's one of Harold's doves, Fluff ... Powder ... I don't know what its name is! It's what he keeps in that cage!" All she could do was stare in horror as the huge black dog's tail disappeared through the bushes. Beside her, Michael's face wore largely the same expression as he started to try and pull loose the feathers that were stuck to his fingers with model glue. Anne came around when she saw her son's appearance and practically yanked him out of his pajamas as she drug him to the bathroom and turned on the shower. "Thank God they're at the market, but you need to wash off every one of those feathers. I'll clean up your room. I guess we'll have to tell him. I'm dreading that. After I get all those feathers up I'll try to call your father and see what he says."

A good hour later when Anne tried to ring her husband, he was away from his desk. He was balancing his rather large girth on top of a small riding mower just outside of Jay Vern Jones's bathroom window. Jay Vern had been in a really good mood ever since he had out-smarted the police the day before and had even come back to his trailer after spending the night at his sister-in-law's for some clothes, what was left of his pot and beer, and to take his monthly shower and shave. He had just tilted his head back and looked down his nose toward the mirror, contorting his mouth to get his upper lip when he saw Officer Frye's pudgy fingers pressed up against the window screen. He dropped to the floor, but the policeman was able to spot him in his underwear, hugging the toilet with shaving cream still on his face.

When Anne was hanging up the phone from the police station, she was startled to hear the television on in the next room. She glanced around the door facing and saw an old rerun of *My Favorite Martian* playing, on television and Slobber sitting in her husband's recliner watching it with the serious manner of a politician counting votes.

"Oh I didn't know anybody else was still here," she said, thankful that it wasn't Harold or one of the Wilcox sisters.

"They said they wouldn't need me there today," he said, never taking his eyes off the television. "That prissy fella said that he didn't want me there, so I just stayed here. What's with all the feathers?" Anne had been staring at the floor and looked up to see him studying her hand where she held some of Fluff/Powder's remains. "Y'all slaughter your own chickens around here do you? Stuffing pillows?"

"Umm, no." Anne pulled her hand back behind her but for some reason she blurted out the truth. "One of the prissy ... Harold's doves flew into the fan upstairs. We were just trying to figure out what to do." Slobber registered it for a second and then let out a sadistic sounding cackle that seemed so out of character for him that Anne had to chuckle herself. Then the laughing stopped just as suddenly as it had started and he went back to watching television just as he was when Anne had come into the room. She just rolled her eyes, threw up her hands and turned to leave when he called her back into the room.

"Say, what was you gonna do? 'Bout the bird, I mean."

"Well I guess that we'll tell Harold the truth. Face the music." He stared back at the TV for a few seconds.

"I wouldn't do that. I mean he's so high strung anyway. Anything happen to those birds he will throw a hissy. Might drop a gasket and keel over right here."

"But I don't see as we have any choice." He thought for a few more seconds, rubbing his chin, and then got up and switched off the TV.

"How 'bout I get something to put in its place? You said those birds are doves. You got woods, fields around here don't cha? I could probably catch you something to pass for the real thing at least until he's gone."

"I don't think that we have white doves running wild around here."

"Well, you got a pet store in town? I'll just ride up there and get one. No big deal." Anne had short conversations with the angel on her right shoulder and the devil on her left, which did little to ease her mind. In the end she simply looked into Slobber's dark, blank, staring eyes, shrugged her shoulders and said, "thanks."

A little later, back up was called to Jay Vern Jones's trailer and an ambulance hauled Officer Leon Schaler to Randolph Memorial Hospital to treat wounds that he suffered in the buttocks from a double shot of rock salt from Jay Vern's shotgun. Jay Vern barricaded himself in his trailer and demanded three cases of Pabst Blue Ribbon, ten thousand dollars cash, a brand new T-Bird and free passage to the Mexican border.

Early that afternoon Michael was messing around by the creek again and heard a bottle of Coke calling him. His mother had not given him leave to go explore the woods because of the mess with Harold's dove. When he left, Slobber was still not back and his mother was nervous to say the least. Anyway he wanted to hang close to see what Slobber brought back and if it would fool Harold.

When he got back to the house he just laid his bicycle down in the driveway and dashed in for the Coke. Slobber and his mother were whispering when he walked into the kitchen and Anne looked relieved to see that he wasn't one of the other guests.

"Everything okay?" he asked his mother.

"Looks good," said Slobber. His mother simply shrugged her shoulders and opened her mouth to say something when the sound of a car roaring into the driveway was followed by the sickening sound of metal scraping metal and similar tones of Harold cursing in the driveway.

"Who in the hell left a bicycle in the driveway?" he yelled as he tore into the kitchen.

"My bicycle," was all that Michael could choke out before he felt his chin start to quiver. He didn't want to say anything else.

"Well you shouldn't have left it in the middle of the driveway! You've just succeeded in tearing up the bottom of my car. Oil's leaking everywhere. Why don't you use your brain next time!"

"Wait just a minute Mr. Harold." Anne broke in, stretching herself to her full five foot two inch height. "That's my son..."

"I don't care if he's the Prince of Wales," screamed Harold as the Wilcox sisters hurried in behind him, "he's ruined my car! My company is paying you a substantial amount for me to stay here! More than you'd get from anyone else for the simple reason that me bringing my babies prevents me from staying in a hotel! This will be docked from the final fee, that is, if you get paid at all and I'll see that you don't if I continue to be treated in this manner!" He stopped for several seconds, face red, chest heaving like he was trying to calm down and when he spoke again his voice was quiet. Strained. Ominous. Clint Eastwood quiet. "What is going to happen now is that I am going to go upstairs, get packed and arrange for repairs to my car. Miss Wilcox, you and your sister will drive me into town if need be, and then take me to High Point so that my company can still salvage a showing with furniture bearing comic book characters and a center piece with a carving from a bad monster movie."

"Godzilla's actually been in 15 movies so far," Slobber stated, apparently oblivious to Harold's tirade.

"Will you please shut up! You have done enough, and I will not tell you again to keep your trap shut! Now," he said turning towards the Wilcoxes, "I will be ready to go in an hour. I advise you to be ready."

Michael went outside to Harold's car and stooping down, looked underneath at his bicycle. It was badly bent at the fork and broken half way up the suicide bar, one end of which was sticking in the bottom of the car, and leaking oil was covering it before running off onto the driveway. He had hardly reached underneath and taken hold of the tire before Harold's voice shrieked down from the upstairs window.

"You get the hell away from my car! Don't you think you've done enough damage for one day!" Then a little quieter like he had turned away from the window, "Brat!"

Michael crept around the corner of the house and crawled underneath the big magnolia before he started crying. In a few minutes his mom reached in and handed him his backpack, filled with sandwiches, potato chips, a Coke and all the stuff that he commonly carried when he went on a long hike into the woods.

"If you want to knock around in the woods, you can, okay?" She took his silence to mean yes and she didn't look in to make sure. He never liked anyone to see him cry and under the circumstances she thought it best if she just brought his stuff, left it, and then went back inside.

Michael felt better before he even got to the creek. He carefully crossed it on a large rock and then crossed the stubble field on the other side. He pushed his way through some thick brush and then drank the Coke as he weaved through the trees where the woods got thinner. He didn't really see much. He stopped to look at an old shack that had fallen down and now lay flat underneath the tin roof and played for awhile on a large oak that had fallen and lay on its side. Some rather recent trash ruined his perception of the woods as a desolate place which hadn't seen a human since at least the end of the Civil War. Regardless, he enjoyed the walk and pushed on until he stepped out into the parking lot of an old curb market that set alongside the road that they usually took into town. He sat down on an old whitewashed tire and started eating his lunch. He had just finished a sandwich and opened the bag of potato chips when Slobber pulled onto the gravel on his scooter.

"Y'all right?" he asked, switching off his scooter. Michael could only nod and he looked down toward his feet as a lump rose in his throat. "Those women told your Mama that they would pay for your bicycle." Michael nodded again and Slobber simply sat on his scooter quiet for a minute or two and then popped up the kickstand. "So, uh, I see you later." As he started to crank up the scooter Michael looked to him and blurted out a question that suddenly came to mind.

"Say. Did you find something to replace Harold's doves?"

"Sure did."

"What?"

"A big ol' wharf rat that I found out behind your shed. I stuck some feathers on it with glue and put him in the cage today before he got back." Michael stared at Slobber, not knowing whether to be shocked or die laughing as he started the scooter and pulled out onto the road right in front of the Wilcox sister's van. Jennifer had to swerve into the other lane to miss Slobber and hit a good sized pot hole. That not only loosened the fillings in their teeth, but loosened the latch on the bird cage and allowed the still feathered rat, who had been terrorizing Fluff since Slobber had first put him in their cage, to slip out, along with the bird, and onto the floorboard.

"You should have hit him," snapped Harold. The sisters glared at each other but kept silent. Michael, who walked to the shoulder of the road to watch them go, noticed that the van slammed on its breaks just as it reached the crest of the hill and then accelerated dramatically, disappearing over the top. That would have been when the rat chased Fluff up Jennifer Wilcox's left leg and got in a fight with him about three inches south of her belly button.

"Son of a bitch!" Jennifer screamed, hitting the brake with her left foot flooring the gas with her right and then releasing the brake to stomp her foot on the floor in hopes of releasing the buzz saw that was rolling around on her girdle. The result was a mile long skid mark and a heart-stopping squeal as the van hit ninety at the bottom of the hill where they passed the city limits sign and proceeded to dart about the downtown area like a top from Hell. Over the next twenty minutes they committed every moving violation on the books for the city of Randleman, the county of Randolph and the state of North Carolina. Had all the police not been at Jay Vern Jones's trailer in a vain attempt to flush him out, the speeders surely would have been charged had they been caught. They succeeded in flying through a bank drive-through the wrong way, the drive-through at the Jitter Burger in reverse and a car wash sideways, without paying. They ran the town's stoplight, took out the Civil War memorial and crashed into, through and out of the liquor store. By the time they had gotten to the Old Railyard Road they had slowed to a mere eighty. They passed the train and then crossed over the tracks in front of it, clearing the front of it by a mere foot. Then they crossed back over the tracks, missing the front of the train by an inch before launching off the embankment that overlooked the Avalon trailer park. In the brief second that they were in the air and the sound of the road under their wheels had been replaced by the wind whistling past their window, Harold did an excellent impression of Little Richard in soprano, Jennifer put her Lee Press Ons through the hard plastic steering wheel, and Dottie, who had not said anything since they arrived, looked at her sister and said a single word that aptly described what Fluff the dove was doing on her head at that moment.

No one was hurt when the van crashed through the back wall of Jay Vern Jones's trailer. Jay Vern was sitting beneath a front window hugging his shotgun dreaming of half naked brown women and alcoholic drinks with umbrellas in them when the back wall pushed in like a trap from a Fu Manchu movie and squirted him out through the window in nothing but cut off jeans and a flip flop.

"Rats," was the last thing that Michael Frye said the last second of the last minute of the last hour of his fourth summer vacation. He did all the things that he had wanted to do. He had explored what he thought was every last inch of the woods. He had ridden his brand spanking new Evel Knievel bicycle, and he and his family had taken both of their annual summer trips—Myrtle Beach and the mountains. The thing was, although he had fun, these things in a way seemed anti-climactic. As he turned off the light on his nightstand, the one with the crab legs, and laid his head down beneath his oaken headboard, the one with Godzilla so beautifully carved into it, he wished that every day of his vacation had been as exciting as the first two.

11

The Brief Reign of Pharaoh Ho-Ho and the Queen of Denial

> This is the script to a play that was inspired by the incident concerning the mummified rat and the homeless man eating the candy off the gingerbread houses.

The Brief Reign of Pharaoh Ho-Ho and the Queen of Denial
A Drama by Jonathan Farlow

NARRATOR: It was a great day to be alive. It was also one of those days where it stunk royally to have to spend it at work. It was December 20th, five days before Christmas, and the weather babe on TV was forecasting for more in a couple of days. The good news was, or so I thought, that the library would be nearly deserted, *(icy footsteps)* but as Rob Baker from the children's room and I slip-slided across the icy parking lot, I could see the usual Internet crowd huddled in front of the main entrance. I had one eye on them and one on my feet as I made my way around a new looking Escalade and just about slid into Marilyn Misenheimer. I said excuse me, but she seemed to be too intent on yelling at her teenage son to notice. There was a large four-door Dodge pickup parked directly behind the Escalade, with a large dent in the front of the truck and the back of the SUV. The rear compartments of each were filled with what looked to me to be garbage. *(Argument sounds)*

NARRATOR: "She's here early, and here I thought today would be a breeze."

ROB: "I know, at least she's not heading to your department."

NARRATOR: "You think she's coming to see you?"

11. The Brief Reign of Pharaoh Ho-Ho and the Queen of Denial

ROB: "Most definitely." *(Key sounds and the sound of unlocking doors and then one opening.)*

NARRATOR: "We open at nine." *(There should be several grumbling voices in the background which should end when the doors shut followed by the sound of people climbing stairs.)*

ROB: "I need to get upstairs and let Gladys know that the 'Divine Miss M' is on her way up. I'll talk to you later."

NARRATOR: "Let me know what happens."

NARRATOR: I went back to my desk, answered my e-mail, went to the bathroom, got a bottled water and by the time I got to the reference desk Marilyn Misenheimer was limping into the children's room, followed by her oldest son Marshall, who looked to be pushing a six-foot Egyptian sarcophagus on a hand truck *(squeaky wheel sound)*. Her younger son Martin was following him carrying what looked at that distance to be a large cake pan. Rob called me a little before lunch to tell me what transpired that morning and apparently it went down like this. The good news is that Gladys was warned, the bad news was that no amount of mental, physical or spiritual preparation could ready her for the sight of a very irritated and haggard-looking Marilyn Misenheimer limping through the door of the children's room followed by her oldest son Marshall wheeling a six-foot Egyptian sarcophagus *(squeaky wheel sound)* on a hand truck, nor her youngest son Martin, the genius, carrying what appeared to be a mummified rat in a casserole dish.

MARILYN MISENHEIMER: "Martin's ancient Egypt project is here for display."

NARRATOR: Gladys could only sit at her desk and look up at Marilyn for a few seconds. She was almost afraid to speak because of Marilyn's disheveled and vexed appearance. It appeared to Gladys that Marilyn had had some sort of accident, or at least a very bad morning. After a fair amount of stammering she was about to get the words out.

GLADYS: "Umm, you were signed up for January. We aren't reserving the children's room during December. The story time group's displaying their gingerbread houses and we're going to decorate for Christmas."

MARILYN MISENHEIMER: "What? I reserved this room in September to display Martin's project this month and here we are. We're a week late. I'm surprised you haven't been calling."

GLADYS: "Let's look at the schedule." *(Sound of a drawer opening and closing and the sound of a plastic binder being laid on the desk and opened.)*

MARILYN MISENHEIMER: "See here. *(Sound of her finger tapping the page several times.)* Here is my signature on the month of December."

GLADYS: "But this month is clearly x'ed out, meaning that this month is not available. The story time group has it to display their..."

MARILYN MISENHEIMER: "Well, you should have been more specific. Martin has his heart set on displaying his project this month. Now you're going to ask him to wait?"

NARRATOR: As if on cue, Martin snorted savagely *(Martin snorts audibly)* in a vain attempt to stifle the deluge of mucus that always seemed to pour from his nose. He looked up at Gladys with that million mile stare of his, which through bottle-bottom glasses made his blue eyes look the size of dinner plates.

GLADYS: "Uh yes, well, I'll tell you what I can do. I can give you the months of January and February. We normally only reserve for a month at a time, but since Martin is so eager to display his project and since he'll have to wait, I'll let him display whatever he wants for the first two months of the new year. I'm sorry for the misunderstanding, but that's the best that I can do."

NARRATOR: Not that Marilyn ever had anything against the Welbourne County school system—well, she did, but she would never admit that—she chose to homeschool Martin. While county schools were good enough for Marshall who, and she did love him dearly, was about as smart as a sack of hammers, she did not feel that the type of person whom our particular school system would hire could scarce do justice for an exceptional child with Martin's intellectual level. No, Martin was small for his age, sickly and asthmatic, but very intelligent. There was no doubt in his mother's mind that when he did take an IQ test, he would register at a genius level. No, Marilyn just couldn't trust her son's education to anyone but herself, and what few tutors she had brought in. Marilyn just stood there, quiet for several seconds, letting Gladys squirm for a moment and then looked down at Martin who was engrossed in the screen saver on one of the card catalog terminals.

MARILYN MISENHEIMER: "Very well."

NARRATOR: While this exchange was occurring Rob was at the reference desk talking to me and speculating as to what was going on between Gladys and Marilyn Misenheimer. He had gone straight into the children's room to let Gladys know that Hurricane Marilyn had blown in, but then took off under the pretext of seeing the business manager concerning the problem with his

11. The Brief Reign of Pharaoh Ho-Ho and the Queen of Denial

dental insurance. In that part he was truthful, because he did intend to see the business manager, who was out sick. After leaving a note on her door, however, he dropped by the reference desk and told me that he'd call back later with an update, but he lingered hoping that the Misenheimers would leave before long. Finally he sucked it up and crept into the children's room just as Marilyn was saying:

MARILYN MISENHEIMER: "Well, come on Martin. Mrs. Finch says that you can't display your project here. I know you're disappointed, but we'll ask Daddy if he can display it in the mill office. Say goodbye and come along."

ROB: "A guilt trip *(Rob whispers)*. Oh give it up."

NARRATOR: Neither librarian would have been surprised if she had whined back to her husband, who was as close as two peas in a pod with Wade Burgess, the county manager, who was, in turn, Elaine Russell, the library director's boss. But to whip out the violins. *(Sad Music)* It was a surprise, but Rob could see that it was working. Everybody who knows Gladys knows that her heart is as big as her belly and it was all too easy for an old battle-ax like Marilyn Misenheimer to use sugar where vinegar had failed and pull Gladys's heartstrings until she got her way.

MARILYN MISENHEIMER: "Martin, let's go. Mrs. Finch is too busy to talk to us. Come on."

ROB: "Stay strong *(Rob whispers)*. Hold your ground."

Fade in rockin' Christmas music and fade out as narrator begins speaking.

NARRATOR: As I was getting back from lunch, Rob flagged me into the children's room. When I got in there, Gladys had just finished stringing Christmas lights up on the sarcophagus.

GLADYS: "There. How's it look?"

ROB: "So, who's he now?" *(Rob chuckles)* "Pharaoh Ho-Ho?"

GLADYS: "Good one."

NARRATOR: "It looks like a drunken soirée at Anwar Sadat's house."

GLADYS: "I know it's tacky, but at least it's festive."

NARRATOR: She stepped back and admired her work for a minute or two and then we all bowed *(trumpet fanfare)* to the regal presence that now stood before us, Pharaoh Ho-Ho.

GLADYS: "Bring that ladder, I've got a Santa beard that'll look cute on the sphinx."

NARRATOR: When Gladys had reluctantly agreed to display Martin's project, she had in mind finding some space for the pharaoh and a table top for the rat and a few other knick-knacks. Maybe a poster showing the life cycle of the ibis or the techniques used in making papyrus, something like that. What she got was an exhibit worthy of the British Museum. This elementary grade level project included, in addition to the rat and the sarcophagi, a four-by-four-by-four foot pyramid which could be entered and where one could view a cut-out of the great pyramid of Giza, complete with a translation of the hieroglyphics. Also, there was a rather imposing bust of the Sphinx which reached the ceiling and was soon to be adorned with a homemade Santa beard. A complete section of the Nile was reproduced in a badly dented and duct taped wading pool, and so many do dads were brought in that it all made the children's room look like a Saturday flea market. Gladys bit her lip as the M's hauled it all in and walked out without a thank you, a how-do-you-do, kiss-my-foot or anything. All she could do after they were gone was look over at Rob, who was returning the same expression, and hum "Joy to the World."

Fade in Christmas music again and fade out as narrator begins speaking.

NARRATOR: Rob was in the process of stapling antlers to the rat, taking time out to spray some of Gladys's Poison perfume on it, himself, and the air around them both to try and cut the stink. Gladys frantically sprayed the air around her with air freshener and talked to Mrs. M on the telephone at the same time.

GLADYS: "Yes Ma'am. I know that I promised to display Martin's Egyptian project through January and I intend to do that, but something has to be done about that rat." ... "Because it stinks. It smells really bad ... I know that Martin followed the exact procedure that the Ancient Egyptians ... I know that he used all reputable sources. You've already told me that, but that doesn't change the fact that it's running everybody out. Yes... Yes... I know... Yes... Okay... Yes, Thank you very much... Well you see... Hello... Hello." *(Sound of a phone being hung up.)* Do you think that the smell would be worth keeping her away?"

Fade in Christmas music again and fade out as narrator begins speaking.

NARRATOR: From the sound that issued from her lips *(horrible sounding gasp)* Gladys and Rob could tell when Marilyn came into the children's room, even though their backs were turned. It started low like a moan that could be heard coming from a crypt at Halloween and rose in pitch and volume until it became a glass splitting wail that Rob was pretty sure could kill dogs at fifty paces. The sound was nothing compared to the sight of the ghoulish apparition that wobbled into the children's room that afternoon and stared at Pharaoh Ho-Ho like a banshee hungry for a soul. Then her eyes, wide with fury, scanned the entire children's room and her mouth worked like a catfish's before she could speak.

MARILYN MISENHEIMER: "Martin's pride and joy!"

NARRATOR: Gladys picked up the rat, and the dish, and approached Marilyn, holding them out in front of her. To Rob it looked like one or both of them was going to draw a gun.

MARILYN MISENHEIMER: "What is the meaning of this? This is a child's project. This is his educational development being turned into a dog and pony show."

GLADYS: "Mrs. Misenheimer, we reserve the right to make any changes to the children's room displays that I see fit. I told you that we couldn't take Martin's project, but you insisted, and in the name of cooperation we took it anyway. I also said that we were going to decorate the children's room for Christmas, and that's what we've done."

NARRATOR: Marilyn just stood there and glared. Nobody in the children's room, including her, could predict what she'd do, but the next movement she made was to hold up her hands like she was giving up, but as she spoke she pointed a broken fingernail at Gladys and jabbed at the air in front of her to emphasize her point.

MARILYN MISENHEIMER: "Oh, I ... that does it, I'm not dealing with you anymore. I am leaving, but rest assured I will be in contact with Elaine Russell. You can bet on that."

NARRATOR: Then she turned to leave, but Gladys called her back.

GLADYS: "Well please take this with you when you leave."

NARRATOR: Marilyn just stood stiff with her back to Gladys. Back straight, legs locked, arms down by her sides and hands in tight fists.

GLADYS: "Mrs. Misenheimer, please take it. It smells and the other patrons have been complaining."

NARRATOR: Marilyn turned on her heel, grabbed the rat by the tail and jerked it toward her. It was then that the tail broke and the rat went sailing across the children's room and hit the big plate glass window *(thump)* between the children's room and the reading area, leaving little gray hairs and a watery yellow substance that sort of splattered *(Group groan in disgust)* and started running down the glass. The rat bounced off one of the low metal shelves underneath the window and fell into a stocking hung in front of a Styrofoam chimney with care that was in turn flanked by clay statues of Horus and Osiris. Mrs. Misenheimer walked to the chimney, fished the rat out, stuffed it into her pocketbook and left looking a lot like someone who had found a nasty surprise in her corn flakes.

Fade in Christmas music again and fade out as narrator begins speaking.

NARRATOR: Gladys had always wanted to take the high road when dealing with troublesome patrons, Marilyn included. She tried to live her life personally and professionally by the Good Book. Regardless, it did her heart good to see the great Marilyn Misenheimer embarrass herself right in the middle of the children's room and stomp out, hopefully for good. She saw it as some sort of victory. She had faced the dragon. She had killed Goliath. That is, until Mitchell Misenheimer came back not an hour after his wife had left. She was not with him, just Marshall, who was wheeling the same dolly *(squeaky wheel sounds)* that he had used to bring everything in that morning. Mitchell set Marshall to work taking everything out and then he asked to see Elaine. No Wade Burgess go-between this time. He wanted to speak to Elaine in person, and when Rob called to let her know he was here, Elaine had him to walk Mr. Misenheimer to her office.

Gladys started to question herself at this point, as we all do when caught playing burr to someone else's saddle. Okay, maybe I wasn't decorating Martin's project just to be festive, she thought, still staring towards the children's room door. Maybe it was a way to beat Marilyn, to prove to her that this is my show and I still have control. Maybe it wasn't the right thing to do. No, it wasn't the right thing to do. Gladys knew that from the beginning. It wasn't the right thing to do, and as soon as Mr. Misenheimer had walked in, that realization plopped down into the pit of her stomach like a lacquered gumdrop. She was so nervous that several times she made excuses to go back to the administrative wing. She needed to go to the storeroom to get more construction paper. She needed to go to the bathroom. She wanted to take a break, but each time Elaine's door was shut and nothing could be heard coming from the other side.

Gladys was standing right there when it opened and Elaine led Mitchell out. He smiled at her and nodded his head cordially before he headed down the hall towards the public area. Elaine was leaving for the day. She already had her hat and coat on and her briefcase in one hand. Reading the anxiety that Gladys had written across her face, Elaine put the other hand gently on her elbow and said:

ELAINE: "Don't worry about a thing."

NARRATOR: It was all Gladys could do to say thank you as Elaine locked her office door. She was answered with a quiet smile and the director headed down the hall as well. It was such a relief. Gladys wasn't going to be fired, or written up, tortured or shot at dawn. The Misenheimers and Wade Burgess weren't going to strap her to the pyramid and beat her with mummified rats. All she could do was go back to the children's room, sit on the corner of her desk and watch Mitchell and Marshall take that stuff away. The only evidence that it had ever been there was the gunk the rat had left on the window. The housekeeper had to scrub for a good half hour with a rag dipped in kerosene for the crud to finally come off, but even today if you look at that window at just the right angle, you can still see a faint stain, almost like a smudge of the Pharaoh's handprint on the glass.

12

Working at the Mayberry Library

I mentioned earlier about Queenie passing away. She had been in pain and had complained about a swollen foot for some time, and we all had been nagging her about seeing a doctor. She had finally decided to go and the last time I had spoken to her in person was a day just like any other. I had said goodbye and left for home. She was absent from work for a long time, and while she was, nobody saw her or went to visit. Remember, Queenie was very particular, even with her appearance, so once she left the library—admittedly she believed that it would be temporary—nobody heard much out of her. Nobody visited her and nobody took her flowers, and that was by choice—her choice. If she was going to greet someone while sick, she would rather not greet them at all.

With Queenie being gone, everything seemed to change; people started leaving, retiring, taking jobs at other libraries and in other fields. For a long time the library, as it had been for so many years, was like the ground. I figured it would always be like this, but alas, it wasn't. I myself joined the exodus. I live three literal minutes away from one of our branch libraries and it had long been a goal of mine to get the director's position at that library. It was a position that I had watched for over a decade. When the lady who had been director there retired, I had applied for and interviewed for that position. I didn't get it, but I kept working at the main branch, all the time looking toward that same library. Years later, just before Queenie got sick, the director retired and Mr. Benz moved into the director's position. That was a given, and the director at the town library moved into his position. That left the town library's director's position open, and I interviewed for it again. Although I didn't get it, that was when Queenie had called. It was the old Catch-22 that I'm sure other people have run into as well. You need a supervisory position to get supervisory experience, and you need supervisory experience to get a supervisory position. I had tried to get the necessary experience other ways—heading committees, teaching martial arts classes, leading story times, etc.—but it never happened for me, and the last time I was turned down for a position as director at our branch I was given another position at that library. It was a lateral move, but it was so close to my house that it was always a plus.

Even though my move to the branch had started with a great deal of disappointment, as soon as I learned that I would be going there anyway, I started looking forward to it. Still, I've always been one to dread change, so there was a combination of exhilaration and hesitation. I've always thought that it was a depressing fact that, as long as I had been at this library, it only took an hour for me to clean out my office and prepare to leave.

I do have to say that the patrons at the branch were wonderful. This is the reason I like living in this particular town. I realize that it has its problems, it's not Mayberry, but it's a lot closer than a lot of places. The people are very supportive of their library, friendly and polite and within a couple of days they made it feel like I had been working there for years. Let me give you an example of this wonderful attitude. Not too long after I had arrived, a regular came up to the front desk and informed me that the bathroom was a mess, which made me think that I was going to have to go in and clean it up, but before I could say anything she went on talking.

"There were paper towels all over the floor. I have never seen such a mess; it was horrible so I cleaned it up." I thanked her profusely because there aren't that many library patrons who would volunteer to clean up a library bathroom.

While I was there I was put in charge of library programming, which is one of the things that I have enjoyed most in my career. I reinstated Family Movie Night where we would show a family friendly movie—that we had licensing for—and provide drinks and popcorn, because what's a movie without popcorn? Pretty soon we had our own regular crowd at Family Movie Night, which saw crowds anywhere from 4 to 50. It was popular and when we would take a break from it, say during the holidays, people were sure to ask when Family Movie Night was coming back. I am glad to say that since I left the branch they have continued Family Movie Night and I hope that the same people have continued to come.

In addition to the Family Movie Night I scheduled various programs that would appeal to different groups of people, promote the library and hope to get some of the people who were not regular attenders of the library to attend as a habit. I tried to have several programs that would focus on seniors. The first program of this type that I scheduled was to have the Medicare coordinator from our county senior adults association come and speak concerning the changes to the Medicare program. I actually got this idea from my parents who were talking while I was over at their house one day about trying to figure out Medicare. Medicare is a very large, very complicated program, and many times it's difficult for those people who need to sign into the program to wade through the red tape and other governmental drivel and figure out which program they need to sign up for. The program was a rousing success. The Medicare coordinator is a very vivacious sweet-natured woman who genuinely cares about the people who are attempting to sign up for these programs and would stay for as long as people had questions and needed assistance. We had her back several times and each time the crowd was great and I think the great majority of them left with most of their questions answered. We also had programs on security at your home and in public by a member of our local police force, container gardening by a couple of master gardeners from the Cooperative Extension Department, and exercise and eating right by staff members from the YMCA and the County Health Department, respectively.

In addition to the more practical programs, I also tried to bring in some that were more entertaining than educational and it was those, along with the Family Movie Nights, that really brought in the people. First, my friend Bones did a program on paleontology. Bones is still one of my closest friends; he is an anatomy professor at Fayetteville State University and a paleontologist. That is, he's one of those lucky people who gets to go out into the desert or somewhere like that and dig for dinosaur fossils. He did three programs at our branch, and turnout was fantastic each time. I guess everybody does love dinosaurs.

> One great story concerning Bones occurred while we were in college. Bones not only has a scientific mind, but a lot of artistic ability as well. One semester he drew a pair of life size Velociraptors mating on his dorm room wall, and yes, they were anatomically correct. The Rabbi was in his room taking pictures of something for the yearbook and accidentally got Bones's dino-porn in the picture. This got him fired from the yearbook staff, which I don't think really hurt his feelings.

We also had a program from a couple of Ghost Hunters, and MUFON, an organization that investigates UFOs. Probably the best-attended program was a lecture by a Bigfoot hunter. The meeting room at the branch has a capacity of 85 people. We were one person away from capacity in the room itself and had people standing in the hall listening to the program through the open door. There were some of our regulars there and others who we hadn't seen before and haven't seen since. They were an unusual bunch of people, most of whom had a story to tell

12. Working at the Mayberry Library

Left to right: Scott, Bones, me and the Rabbi at a Super Bowl party. We were doing our version of "See no evil." Scott had a few cocktails that night.

and most of these stories started with the words, "well we had been drinking a little bit." This was the only library program where I had to cut people off from asking questions and insist that we close the program. At one county staff meeting Mr. Benz announced that in the first year that I took over programming at the branch, attendance went up 115 percent.

In the two years I was there, only one patron sticks out in my mind as being particularly nutty, in a bad way. I think it was during my two week's notice, I can't be sure but I was close to leaving for a new job. A woman came in, her teenage son in tow. She had received a notice in the mail that they owed money for a copy of *Hunger Games* which she proceeded to dispute with the manager. She claimed that they had dropped it in our book drop and that the box must have "ate it." Most library book drops are the same in function as your corner mailbox. A patron drops a book in the slot, it drops into a little holding area underneath and a librarian will periodically empty it and take the books inside to be checked in. In short, there is no way the box could have eaten the book and the director told her this.

She eventually paid for the book with a twenty dollar bill. After the director handed her a receipt for the transaction she jerked it out of his hand and said, "I hope you like that twenty! I wiped my butt with it!" Then she stomped out with her son in tow. After she was gone the director looked over at me and said that he always wiped his butt with hundreds.

13

Potty Humor in the Library

Since we essentially live in an "R-rated" society, I guess it shouldn't be any surprise that a position that deals with the general public would have the occasional R-rated episode. I have heard stories similar to these from EMTs, firemen, nurses, policemen, people who work in social services, even in professions such as meter readers and exterminators. Another thing you can add to librarianship is that it's still a profession (that is, the great majority female.) When I was in graduate school the ratio was around 80 percent. I would expect that the percentage these days is a little lower, but it's still a field that is overwhelmingly female. On top of that, it is a service organization and there are a lot of very conscientious people who work as librarians. There is a possibility that men who come in to the library might misconstrue this friendly demeanor and get it into their heads that there is something between them and the librarian romantically or even sexually. Furthermore, some of our male patrons are regulars and the more they come in, the more familiar I think they become with the staff and the more comfortable they become in being themselves. So they probably feel that they could say something or get away with something more than they could with, let's say, the woman who works at the DMV. Also, the kind of man who would say something or do something harassing or lewd might think that, because there are mostly women around, he might get away with it, or that nobody would be willing to confront them and the staff would just put up with it. I work with a majority of women, and probably way more than half of the people I have worked with have been women. A lot of them, if not all, have, at one time or another, had to deal with the unwanted attentions of a male patron, or had to deal with a situation like some of the ones listed below, which were, other than the events that I witnessed personally, told to me by other librarians.

One very non-descript day I left the Genealogy Room and headed up the stairs to take a break, when I was called back. I turned to see an extremely obese old man sitting on one of the benches just inside the front door. He was leaning back against the wall with one hand on the butt of a wooden cane like a reigning monarch in some sort of bad science fiction movie. His face was red, he was sweaty and his mouth hung open like he was catching flies. He motioned me over and asked for the key to the men's room which was mere feet away. The thing is, policy dictated that the only people who were allowed to use the downstairs bathrooms were patrons that were using the Genealogy Room or the meeting room across the lobby. I knew that he hadn't been in the Genealogy Room and there wasn't an event in the meeting room, so I readied myself to say no, but not long before that the director of the library had told me that rules were rules but to use common sense. As heavy as he was there was no way he was going to get up the stairs. The elevator was about twenty to thirty yards down a hall and I was pretty sure that he wasn't going to make it there either. Shoot, I doubt he could even stand in the shape he was in, so I went back inside the Genealogy Room, told the head of the room the situation and received the men's room key. The man thanked me profusely and I headed upstairs to take my break.

When I got back from my break, I could tell that something was amiss. The head of the room was obviously shaken up and the cleaning lady, who was standing nearby, shared a similar countenance. What I was able to piece together was that a few minutes after I had gone, the head of the Genealogy Room had heard screaming coming from the men's room, which shared a very thin wall with the Genealogy Room. If it had been screams of pain, then I would have suspected that big boy had trouble dropping his payload, but, apparently it was screams of ecstasy. They went on for several minutes and then stopped. In a minute another man, a local homeless man whom we all knew as a regular patron, brought the key back. The cleaning lady said that she had gone into the men's room and had found evidence of their little romantic tryst. The lady who oversaw the Genealogy Room is a dear sweet woman and was profoundly embarrassed by the whole affair in the men's room. Try as we might, we never could get her to say specifically what was being yelled in the next room, but I suspect it was quite foul. As time passed, we—including the Genealogy Room supervisor—had a good chuckle out of it, and some of us have been chuckling about it ever since. The maintenance department even got in on the merriment the next day when they came into the Genealogy Room asking about a work order to have romantic music piped into the men's room next door.

Public restrooms are a little sketchy and I always have at least a small amount of apprehension when I go into one, including the one in the library. You never know what you're going to see, hear or smell. It could be a homeless man taking a bath or a haiku written on the wall in various bodily fluids.

A friend of mine is the director at a branch library in a nearby city. He said that one day a female co-worker came into his office and informed him that a patron had seen a naked man in the men's room. That's another thing you are in danger of seeing in public restrooms; flashes—or sometimes lingering looks at body parts you have no interest in seeing—but this man was stark naked. Now, when you are a male librarian, it's pretty much a given that you work with mostly women, which means that if there's anything amiss in the men's room, you have to take care of it. My friend got up from his desk and went into the men's room. Sure enough, there was a completely nude man in there, his clothes lying nearby. "Sir," he said, trying to summon up an authoritarian tone, which is hard when you are speaking to a naked man, "You either have to put your clothes on or leave." "Okay," the man said, without skipping a beat. He picked up his clothes and walked out, still as naked as the day he was born. He very casually made his way through the crowded library, across the busy parking lot and down the street, which is one of this town's major thoroughfares.

> Contrary to popular belief, Thomas Crapper did not invent the flush toilet. He was a real person, that was his real name and he was a plumber. He did help to popularize the flush toilet and helped develop a couple of related gadgets, such as the ballcock which is that round floaty thing in the tank of your toilet that rises with the water level and closes off the drain when it gets high enough. Some of the first toilets go back to the third millennium and the city of Mohenjo-Dao in modern-day Pakistan, which had some of the most advanced toilets for the day (circa 2800 b.c.). Public toilets were common in Rome (oh, those Romans and their plumbing), often in the vicinity of bathhouses. In the Middle Ages they fell out of favor, I guess they had more important things to worry about. Then in the 18th century they saw a resurgence, sort of a Great Latrine Renaissance, first in Paris, then in Berlin and London.

The same librarian told me another story which, again, involves nudity. The disturbing part of this tale is that it happened in the reading room, the public area, in front of God and everybody, and not in the privacy of the bathroom. He said that they had a group of fellow librarians visiting the library. Sometime after they returned from their lunch break they decided to sit down and go over some things from a meeting they had had that morning. Rather than go into the meeting room, they just took a free table in the reading room and convened. Sometime during the meeting an older woman walked up to them wearing a raincoat. (Do you see where this is going?) "You want some of this?" she purred as she opened her coat to reveal a very wrinkled, very sagging, very naked body.

Getting back to bathroom topics, I sat down with a former co-worker of mine and I told him the story of the naked man in the bathroom that I had heard from my other friend. He told me a whole slew of stories concerning bathrooms, poo and the library. He began his tale by relating to me the story of the Phantom Pooers. He said that it started mere weeks after he had been working in the library when someone found a Walmart bag containing a pair of underwear covered with a thick layer of crap. This was enough to shake anybody, but as it turns out the Phantom Pooer, or Pooers, would be serial perpetrators. They would find the same bags containing underwear caked with feces shoved into the trash can in the men's room. The staff began wandering into the men's room after every use, to try to narrow the list of culprits down to the actual perpetrator. Then it stopped, just like the Zodiac Killer or Jack the Ripper. The Phantom Pooers just stopped without being nabbed. The disappearance of the P.P. did coincide with the cessation of a patron who was no doubt homeless and had become the culprit. My comrade in arms said that for an entire year the Phantom Poopings stopped, but they have since returned.

He went on to tell me that they have found hulking turds in the bathroom, not always in the toilet bowl, however some have been clogged with specimens that looked like they belonged to a hippo. They even found a lone turd on the steps leading to the entrance of the main section of the library. My friend did some investigation (this is really his forte) since he's sort of like the Sherlock Holmes of dung. He could tell which direction the pooer was facing, by the way the end of the turd had been pinched off. And it was clear that the pooer was still in the library. STILL IN THE LIBRARY! Why does this remind me of that scene in *When a Stranger Calls* when Carol Kane gets word from the police that the threatening phone calls she has been getting are coming from inside the house?

They still aren't sure if the Phantom Pooer is one person or multiple people, but the more you think about it the more disturbing it gets. You would think that if someone were to drop a deuce on the front steps of the library they would just leave in embarrassment or, even try and clean it up, not go and plop down at an Internet computer or go look for that Jane Austen novel they've been looking for. What disturbs my friend the most is that there is somebody out there who gets off on taking a dump in the library, or, even worse, doesn't think that it's a big deal to let it fall where it plops.

He said that they thought briefly they had found the culprit. There was a local drunk who would get so sloshed, he would occasionally forget to get up from where he was sitting and go to the john to take care of himself. One day, he came into the library with a bleeding scalp wound from a fall, and trousers full of poo, but the cleaning lady, who is no one to be trifled with, was able to chase him back out again and someone called the police. Since then the man in question has gotten sober and cleaned himself up. Then the pooings stopped for a little while and the staff pinned them on the former drunk, but they have started again and our detective is hot on the trail of the Phantom Pooer.

Another librarian told me about a patron who would call their library on a regular basis, this being several years ago. It was obvious that he was mentally challenged and had a person or people prompting him. He would call, sometimes daily, but at least several times a week and ask a question very innocently and draw snickers and guffaws from whoever was listening in the background. He always asked questions of a sexual nature. The librarians on duty would always answer his question as professionally as they could, trying to keep their voice down so as not to offend another patron who happened to overhear. "What is a condom?" the patron might ask. "How do you use one?" The patron kept calling and these intrepid librarians would keep answering his questions no matter how outrageous they were. One afternoon one librarian decided that she wanted to punk the other one so she got her cell phone out of her purse and snuck off into a corner where she wouldn't be seen from the reference desk. "What is fellatio?" the prankster said, trying to sound as much like their regular caller as she could. "Just a minute," the second said, who got out the dictionary and started reading the definition very clearly and rather loudly. When she realized what it was she was reading, she shouted into the phone, "I will not tell you that!" and hung up. I guess everybody has their limits.

One library had a couple of regular patrons who came in dressed in wedding regalia. Why they were dressed in this manner nobody has seemed to be able to find out. Not too long after their nuptials, the couple disappeared and were gone for an extended period of time. When the woman returned the library staff was quick to ask her where she had been. She told them that she had surgery and had been convalescing for some time. This is a small town library where the librarians know most of their patrons quite well and the librarians began asking about her well being and fishing for details concerning her surgery. "Oh, it's nothing that serious," the lady assured them. "I got breast implants." Before the staff could say anything further she showed the staff her new additions. They were still bandaged but left little to the imagination.

A children's librarian had been on the job for only a couple of weeks and was conducting one of her first story times. As she was telling her tale, she looked down and some of the little girls sitting in the group were giggling, turning red and pointing to one of the little boys sitting nearby. The librarian looked over and saw that the little boy had taken out his "little friend" and was furiously scratching it. "Honey," the librarian said calmly, "You need to do that in your private time, not here during story time." At that point the little boy put everything away and looked up at her with a face that would have been at home on any angel.

Another librarian was waiting on a male patron. At the time, she was pretty far along in her pregnancy, and apparently this was obvious. After awhile the man said: "I have something to tell you but you'll probably get mad." "Well no," this brave soul responded, "go ahead." "No, you'll get mad." "No I won't, what would you like to say?" "No, No, No." "Please, go ahead." "You have a body most women would die for."

The same librarian was still in the late stages of her pregnancy and was waiting on two teenage girls when one said, "Can I ask you something?" Remembering the gentleman's compliment about her body the librarian very hesitantly agreed to answer the young lady's question. "Are you a nun?" At this question both the librarian and the young lady's friend said, "What?" "She's pregnant." The friend said, "Yeah, but I thought that she might have been excommunicated."

Things Librarians Would Love to Say to Their Patrons

1. Hello, welcome to the library. We would love to help you in any way we can, but some thinking will be required.
2. We would like to remind you that you will be sharing space with other human beings including us. Please bathe and take care of other hygienic chores before entering our facility.
3. We realize that we have a great deal of attractive young ladies working here, but please keep in mind that they are in no way interested in you romantically.
4. Screaming, cursing and threatening us will make your overdue fines go up.
5. Two minutes before we close is not the time to type a résumé, read War and Peace or teach your extremely shy child responsibility by having him or her tell us what they want.
6. Yes, we know you are a taxpayer, but some services, copies, printouts, overdues and the like may cost. Rest assured we are not part of a larger government conspiracy that is out to bleed your bank account 10 cents at a time.
7. No, we do not know your e-mail password and we will not call Yahoo.
8. Please speak in complete sentences. Just throwing your library card across the desk and grunting doesn't tell us anything.

14

Goodbye

As rewarding as my time at our branch was, it turns out I wasn't there for very long. One day my wife was in the library surfing the Internet for a job herself and found an opening in a library in a nearby county. She printed it out, gave it to me and told me to at least consider it. I'll be truthful when I first glanced at the notice that she had given me, I blew it off and it laid on my desk for the rest of the day. I knew at that point that the county system I had been in for almost two decades was my home and that was where I would retire. I worked with great people. I lived within walking distance from work, although I never did walk to work. I never got the chance because of having to haul my kids to school in the morning. I worked in the town I lived in and it's the place where I live now and I truly love living there. However, was I satisfied? As I looked back on it, if I'm honest with myself, no I wasn't. I liked the people I worked with, I liked the patrons and I liked the library. Still I felt that I didn't want to stop there. I felt that I had more to give to the profession. I think I had more talent than the job entailed. I wasn't happy and a couple of times it reflected badly on my job performance.

I owe so much to my wife. Remember, it was her who talked me into taking the temporary position which turned into my career. She also dared me to start writing because I was complaining about a book I had read and didn't like and she told me that if I thought I could do better I should give it a try. She has fished manuscripts from where they were wadded up in a drawer or thrown into the trash. If it wasn't for her, you wouldn't be reading this, she's responsible. On top of all that and much more, she didn't let me drop the notion of applying for this new job and, once again, she won out and I applied for the position not really expecting to hear back. I applied in the morning and my wife and kids and I were eating at our favorite restaurant when my cell phone rang. It was the director of

14. Goodbye

the library calling me in for an interview. My family was thrilled, I was nervous. The whole thing sort of produced a duality of emotions. I was scared that I wouldn't get the job and I would disappoint my family. I was also scared that I would get it and I would have to venture out from the relative safety of the system I had grown up in and matured in and venture out into whole wide world.

When I went in for the interview I had decided that I would give it everything I had and really tried to sell myself. When it was done I felt okay with it. It went okay but still I had my apprehensions. One thing I hate about job interviews—and having been on the other side of them I know that nothing can be done about it—is that I wish you could get some sort of clue as to how you did right then. I would much rather have an interviewer tell me that I suck instead of spending the time wondering before getting that thin little envelope in the mail. The word was a little slower in coming because I had interviewed just before Christmas, so I had to wait through the Christmas holiday, and by a few days after we got back I was at the stage where I was convinced I didn't get the job and, despite my apprehension in even applying, I spent my time wondering what I had done wrong. What was so wrong with me that I had wasted a good chunk of my life in a profession I truthfully shouldn't have even pursued? I think I was still in this type of mindset when my future supervisor called and offered me the job.

My new job was not without its growing pains. If you stay in one place as long as I did, you develop a habit for doing things one way, and then you have to forget what had been drummed into your head at the other place and relearn it a new way. Still, I really like this job and finally, at long last, I am a supervisor. Is it everything I thought it would be? Well sort of, and more, when you are a supervisor and someone calls in, guess who might be called upon to cover? You. When a patron gets irate when he is charged $32.55 because he turned in an audiobook that was missing a disc and swears up and down that he checked and all the discs were there, but in reality it's under the seat of his truck covered in crayon marks, dust bunnies and a thin layer of Johnny Walker Black whiskey, guess who gets to iron out all that stuff? That's right. A supervisor does. Still, I like being involved with the administrative side of library work, one of the few departments that I had never worked in.

I guess in the back of my mind for some reason I expected the new place to be low key and laid back like the branch where I had worked previously, since this was also a small town library, larger than the branch but smaller than the library where I had worked for years. It is a stone's throw from the town where I had worked and presently live. No dice. There are still those strange patrons I have been speaking of throughout this book at the new library, and these people, like those at the larger library, tend to be a little more fiery than people at the last place. Most people who come into this library are fine, polite and industrious, but there are some people who seem like they're from the dark side of the moon. It's like leaving Mayberry and moving to Twin Peaks. I wasn't there too long before a patron got upset over some money he owed for photocopies. He had made them and claimed that he meant to pay, but didn't have any cash on him. He wanted me to put the cost of the copies on his library card, like you would do for a fine or a similar charge. This is a practice the previous library where I worked had allowed. At this new library, however, it was not policy to do this, and that is what I'm beholden to enforce, so I informed him that I couldn't put the charge on his card but I would hold the copies for as long as it would take for him to get the appropriate amount of cash or bring a check. I said that we would hold the materials for the next couple of days. At that point this guy got hotter than a match and started screaming at me like someone hadn't done in quite a while. He chastised me for not trusting him and announced that he was a man of integrity. Then he called me a socialist, which is funny on several different levels. If I was working for a governmental institution that was socialist, why would he even have to pay for his copies? Do socialist regimes even have programs that give the populace free access to information? Probably not. Also, in speaking of me personally, and you can talk to the people who know me, I am not a socialist. Nowhere close.

I stood my ground and the fellow ended up leaving, after taking my name, without his copies. Just a couple of minutes after he left I was talking to one of my co-workers, who had also dealt with him, and he came back in carrying a watch. He had found it on the sidewalk outside the building and he handed it to my co-worker. "Give it to him," he said gesturing toward me with his thumb. "He probably needs it." I don't know what he meant by that but he left again without any further comment. He has been in the library since then, but I have not talked to him or assisted him in any way. We held his copies for quite a while in case he still wanted them, but he never came back for them.

One of the things I love about being in my present position is the hiring. It's not so much the interview process but the fact that we're actually changing somebody's life for the better by giving them a job. After we interview some people for a job and we make a decision about who we want, I always want to call them right then to start immediately, but there is paperwork and other odds and ends to take care of, but I am on pins and needles until the new person starts.

My supervisor and I were in our conference room interviewing a very professional, well-dressed young lady who was seeking a full-time position at our library. The whole thing was going on really well when we heard a great deal of yelling out in the library. The door was closed but we figured the people on duty could handle it, so we pushed on with the interview. A few seconds later one of our co-workers busted in like Kramer on *Seinfeld*. We were told that there was a situation that needed our attention, so we stepped out into the library and were greeted by a sight that was reminiscent of the last chopper out of Saigon. The library was already crowded and patrons were being forced to jump out of the way and throw themselves up against the shelves as a gang of people, made up mostly of teenage, or early twenties young men, who were chasing a small wormy looking fellow, with a long white t-shirt and a tattoo on his face. While they were trying to run this guy down, a very short heavy set woman, who I assumed to be their mother, had hold of the guy's shirttail yanking back on it for all she was worth trying to slow him down. The whole time she was screaming, "This is a citizen's arrest!" She sounded a lot like Gomer Pyle from *The Andy Griffith Show*. Our co-worker had the foresight to call the police, but in the time between the call and the arrival of the authorities, the guy ran out the door, almost bowling over a woman with a baby carriage as they went, with his pursuers right on his heels. We all went outside and watched the entire crowd run the guy down and slam him up against the door of the Baptist church across the street. When a patrol car did arrive, the officer flew out of the car and dispersed the crowd before they could do any permanent damage to their quarry, leaned him against the hood of his car, frisked him and then put him inside.

From what we were able to ascertain the guy had broken into the family's house. Yes, all the people who were chasing him were from a single family and he did have warrants out for his arrest. When the family saw him in the library they called the police, which was the logical thing to do, but instead of simply watching him or making sure the fellow didn't leave, they decided to tackle him in the middle of a crowded library. I don't think anybody was injured during the melee, but the security arms that are situated at the entrance and try not to allow people to exit on that side were badly bent from where about 1,000 pounds of humanity plowed through them going in the wrong direction.

As the police were hauling the perpetrator away the director tried to explain to the mother why this had not been the most advisable course of action, but she would not be dissuaded, redneck logic being what it is. We went back to the meeting room and our interviewee was still where we left her. "Are you sure you want to work here?" I asked her, jokingly. "Oh yeah. Absolutely." And she finished the interview with aplomb and grace as if nothing had ever happened. As stressful as situations like this have been, they have helped soothe the trepidation of moving into a new library system. I have laughed a lot at them and it still helps me to feel that, although I'm in a different library system, some things in the field never change, and that helps me feel a definite connection to the place where I worked for so long.

Appendix A: Library Stories

The following are stories collected by the author from librarians who experienced them.

An ever vigilant librarian noticed a man stick something down the front of his pants and head for the exit. He chased the individual down the steps to the entrance where he caught up with him. The librarian was somewhat taken aback because he didn't think the situation warranted calling the police, but as conscientious as he was being, he did not want to reach down the man's pants to retrieve whatever he had there. Before he could act the man said, "I know what you're thinking. You think I stole a library book. I promise it's a bottle of liquor."

A patron walks into a library first thing in the morning and looks around like he was lost. Every librarian has seen these looks and they were never funnier for me than when they would come into the Genealogy Room, which only had one entrance. When they would leave, they would get that look on their face and head toward the closet door and have to be pointed to the exit. The patron in this library asks for the elevator. "We don't have one," the librarian replies. "Well how do you get to the second floor?" "We don't have one."

A man came into a library and made photocopies. He reached into his pocket to retrieve some cash, and when he pulled his hand out, a pair of women's panties wafted to the floor and were quickly snatched up by the man and stuffed back into his pocket before he hurried toward the exit.

One library was having trouble with patrons stealing toilet paper out of the bathroom so the head of the lending department had a security sticker put in each roll, you remember those right? Within a couple of hours the security gates

Appendix A: Library Stories

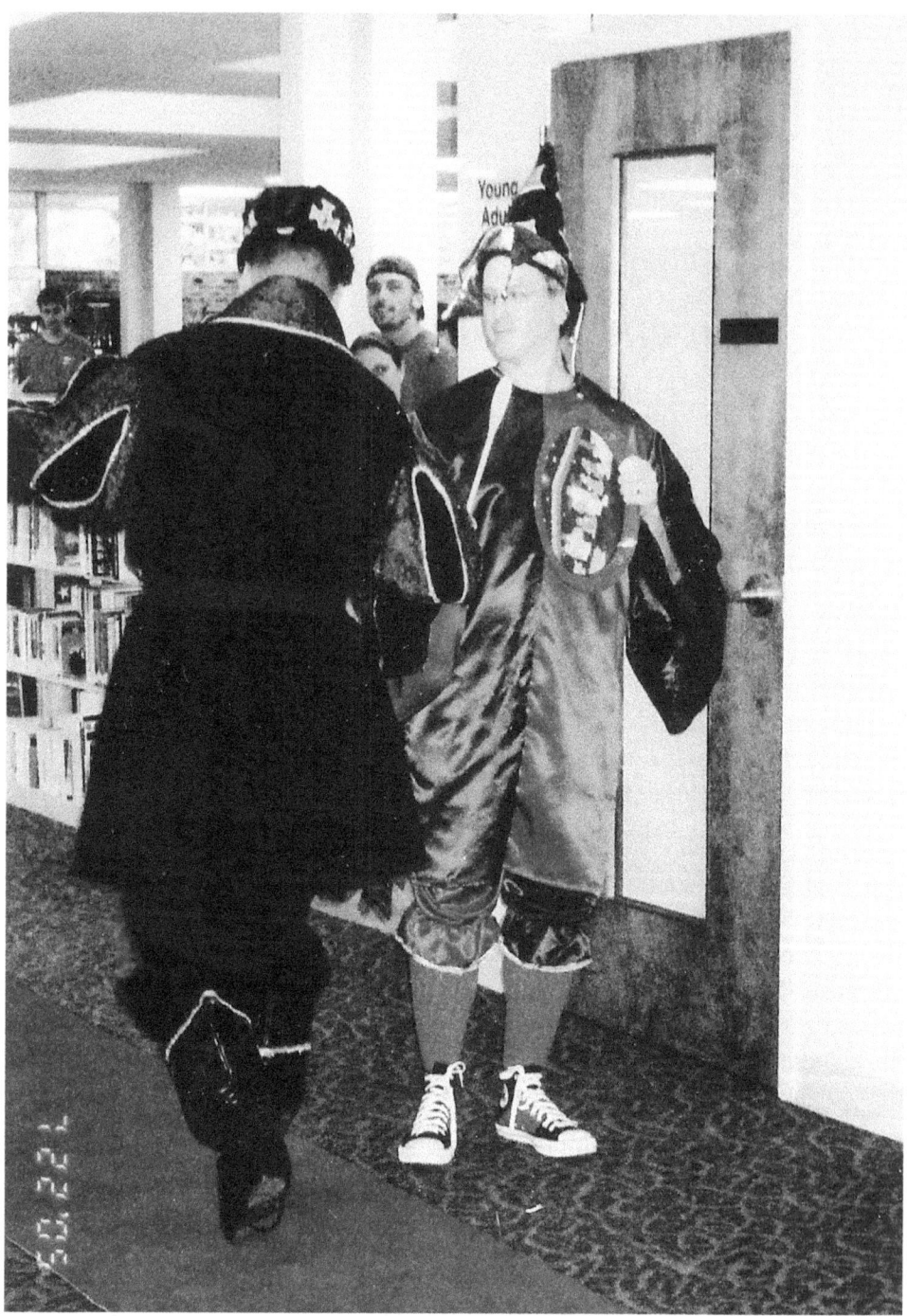

I truly did everything at the library: reference, A/V, genealogy and even a stint as the library jester. (The king is Doug Nixon.)

sounded and the head of lending, a very Queeniesque woman, so I'm told, charged out from around the desk and simply said. "Give it here." When the patron didn't respond immediately she held out her hand and snapped her fingers. They both stood where they were for a few more seconds and then the patron handed the toilet paper over.

A reference librarian said that a very scary individual walked into their library one night. He was wearing a black t-shirt paying homage to someone along the lines of Marilyn Manson. He had long stringy hair, which was an aberrant shade of black, several piercings and a multitude of tattoos. His reference question did nothing to ease the librarian's concerns. He asked about the effects of formaldehyde on the human body. Despite his misgivings the librarian did his best to answer the man's question. As it turns out the patron had a legitimate reason to ask such a question. He had a young child and lived in an old mobile home. Mobile homes of that era are made of materials that release formaldehyde into the air as they decompose. This concerned father wanted to make sure that no harm was coming to his young son.

One busy morning a librarian was assisting patrons in signing in on the Internet. When one lady's name was called she started announcing that she couldn't find her phone. The librarian helped the lady look, but they couldn't find it until they called the next name. A very large woman who had been sitting in a chair nearby stood up and started toward the computers, giving the reference desk a view of the first lady's phone wedged in the crack of the second lady's backside. The phone clattered to the floor unbeknownst to the lady whose backside it had formerly occupied. Too bad the first lady didn't get a call while the phone was wedged in there. I would have liked to have seen the big lady's face when the phone buzzed.

A librarian, who was engrossed in something at the reference desk, looked up and straight into the large breasts of a woman who had just walked up and laid them on the counter like a couple of watermelons. She was wearing a halter top which barely covered her assets and started pulling things out of her substantial cleavage. Cell phone, wallet, Kleenex, 12 head of cattle, a 1961 Camaro, a family of four, you know, the usual thing. Then she reached in, pulled out a couple of dollar bills and handed them to the librarian to pay for her photocopies, who made it a point to say that they were warm and damp.

In the first few years of libraries accessing the Internet, a particular library had only a couple of Internet stations for use by the public. This same library had a rather unusual patron. He was a Vietnam veteran and, I'm sorry to say, was affected greatly by what he went through when he was in the armed services. He was very excitable, unpredictable and, more often than not, came in drunk. The favorite rant of this rather irascible character was the fact that he was not getting the benefits due him for his time serving his country. According to him, the reason he was not getting his benefits was because he was listed as Missing in Action. Obviously he was not missing in action because, at least once a week he was standing in the library ranting about his benefits. During one visit he rather bluntly demanded some help on one of the Internet computers. He wanted the librarian to basically hack into the Department of Defense's website and change his record so that he would get his benefits. If you know anything at all about computers you know how ludicrous an idea like this is. On this particular day, as was his custom, this patron was extremely inebriated and he kept leaning all over the librarian and, semi-accidentally, groping her as he was directing her on the computer. Finally the librarian told the patron that she had another idea that might help him. Then she went back to the reference desk and asked another librarian on duty to call the police. While the police were on the way, the man kept sitting at the computer and the other librarian got a rather large dictionary and stood guard behind the patron, prepared to beat him over the head with the Funk and Wagnalls, until the police got there.

A librarian I myself worked with was at the lending desk when a young man walked up wearing a wool ski cap that was smoking vigorously, almost like the Tinman's hat. The librarian informed him that he was on fire, to which he replied, "Well, thank you very much." He poked out his chest and puffed up like a peacock, thinking that the librarian has just complimented his virility.

"No," the librarian insisted. "You're smoking; you're going to catch fire." She pointed to his hat and the fellow put himself out before anybody actually saw flames. From what she was able to piece together, he was outside smoking and when he headed inside he put his cigarette out on the bottom of his shoe and stuck it under his hat. It wasn't out all the way, so the hat started smoldering.

At the library where I am employed, the public Internet computers can be logged off from the reference desk. At other libraries they are on timers and set to go off shortly before the library closes. When libraries first started offering Internet access, however, it all had to be done manually. The patron would come in and the librarian would take him or her to the computer and enter in a password or something along those lines. Then when the patron was done, the computers had to be manually logged off, the same for closing time. Each public computer had to be logged out and then turned off for the night. One librarian was performing this procedure and when she sat down in a chair to log off a computer, the smell of stale urine hit her nose, followed by a growing wetness spreading across her

Appendix A: Library Stories

bottom. Her response is exactly the same as it would be for most of us. "Ahhhh-hhhhhh!" Then she left, immediately.

At present, in addition to the face to face method, librarians can communicate with their patrons through the mail, by e-mail and even via chat room, but for years the ultimate in high tech communication in the library world was the telephone. When you're talking about funny and unusual instances in the library, the phone gives it a new angle because you can't see the person but you can still hear their voice, and for some reason that just adds humor to it. If you're old enough you can remember Bob Newhart's comedy routines where he is talking on the phone and you can only hear his side of the conversation. It wouldn't be as funny if you heard the other side. Anybody can call the library and some patrons do on impulse. It's easy, and most librarians I've talked to have had a patron that would call a multitude of times a day with some little question or tidbit of information and it was pretty evident that they were just lonely and wanted somebody to talk to. One thing, I think, that adds to the humor is that when people are on the phone, they are at home and are comfortable enough to be more themselves than if they were standing in front of you in a public place. We've all gotten that call from a harried parent with what sounds like a riot going on behind them and them stopping the conversation every two seconds to scream behind them for everybody to shut up.

I hadn't been at the library too long when I was helping a lady on the phone who was looking for information on the balalaika, which is a Russian instrument resembling a guitar with a triangular body. Mr. Duncan was hanging around behind me, and the minute he heard me say "balalaika," he started dancing around saying balalaika-laka-laka-laka-laka-laka-laka. I burst out laughing, but I was able to get the transaction done and I apologized to the lady as Duncan's little dog and pony show continued behind me.

The reference desk phone rang at the library and when the attending librarian picked up the phone the patron on the other end asked her what to do if you had a horse on your porch.

A couple of years ago the state library's slogan for the library system of North Carolina was "the very best place to start." At one library the management wanted its librarians to work the state library's slogan into their phone greeting. It went something like this: "Thank you for calling the _____ public library, the very best place to start, we're your home for education and information. How may I help you?" One day one of the librarians was in a hurry, picked up the phone and flubbed the greeting. "Thank you for calling the _____ public library, the very best place to fart." The rest of the greeting was lost, as both the librarian and the patron burst out laughing.

A librarian picked up the phone and the lady on the other end asked what kind of caterpillar was attached to her husband's arm. She could hear the husband moaning in the background.

A librarian received a call asking if the planet "Nebula" existed. While she had the librarian on the phone he proceeded to get into an argument with another person, both being extremely intoxicated, over whether or not the planet "Nebula" exists. FYI, there is not a planet called "nebula." A nebula is an interstellar cloud of dust, hydrogen, helium and other ionized gases.

The same librarian answered a call where the patron asked her to catch her up on all the soap operas. When I was at my previous place of employment I worked about 10 minutes from my parents' house. I ate lunch with them every work day and we would watch *The Young and the Restless* and *The Bold and the Beautiful* together. I guess I could have brought them up to speed on those two.

One night the phone at a small town library rang, and when the librarian picked up the phone it was a lady who lived across the street. "There's a lady in the shop next door to you." It was a beauty shop. "She's in there by herself and a man just went in. I was wondering if there's somebody there who could go check on her." "He might be a customer." "Well he's a Mexican." "Um uh, still he might be a customer or maybe a friend of hers. If it looks like something is wrong over there we'll call the police. You keep watch and do the same, okay?"

One of the earliest pieces of advice I was given in the library profession was that we are not in the position of offering advice. We don't offer medical advice, legal advice, tax advice or any kind of advice, we just provide the materials to let the patron shape their own opinion concerning the matter. You would think that it would be easy, but every so often you got one of those patrons who was itching to get an answer to a medical or legal problem and would not let it go unless somebody, even you—a total stranger and not a doctor or an attorney—gave him that piece of information. I've told patrons before that I am not qualified to give that kind of advice, it is unfair to the patron and it would be illegal. Most will accept this, but still there are some who will keep digging.

 A librarian answered the phone one night and the lady on the other end said, in a very thick country accent, "Do you reckon I got blocked bowel?" "Excuse me?" the librarian says, because if someone says something that random, you always have to ask for a little clarification. "Do you reckon I got blocked bowel?

I mean I haven't gone since Monday." The librarian was getting the call on a Thursday. "Do you reckon I got blocked bowel?" "Well ma'am," the librarian responded, "I'm not really qualified to say, but let me look up something on what you are looking for." "Well do you reckon I got blocked bowel?" The librarian got the appropriate book, this was before the Internet was widely available, and read the symptoms to the patron. There was a few seconds of silence and then the patron asked, "Do you reckon I got blocked bowel?"

The same librarian answered the phone on another night and the woman on the other end started the conversation with, "My husband thinks that I have menopause. What do you think?"

"Well, I'm not really qualified to say. Let me look up something for you." "Well okay, but my husband is saying that as moody as I've been lately that I must be going through menopause." The librarian was off the phone for a couple of minutes and then she returned with a medical encyclopedia. "Let me read through the symptoms for you." Every symptom the librarian read, the woman had experienced. "Are you experiencing hot flashes?" "Well yeah, a little." "Insomnia?" "Yeah, well I haven't slept worth anything in years." "And you mentioned irritability?" "Yeah, my husband says that I'm a bear." The librarian continued to read through the list of symptoms, and when she got to the last one she had to chuckle and think for a bit on the best way to present this to the patron. Finally she cleared her throat and just put it out there. "So, uh, are you growing a beard?" The lady on the other end of the phone burst out laughing and continued snickering for a couple of minutes at least. As soon as she calmed down enough she answered the librarian's question. "Yes I am."

When I was at my hometown library Mr. Benz was at the reference desk and someone walked up to him and stuck a Styrofoam cup in his face with a bug in it. "Do you know what this is?" the guy asked as Benz jumped back. As my co-worker thumbed through the bug guides, he was able to find out that it was an assassin bug, that it was poisonous, and that it was a spreader of Chagas disease which is potentially deadly to humans.

> This story was inspired by various events that occurred in the library, most of which I have already related in earlier chapters, namely the story of Mr. Benz and the assassin bug.

The Ghost of Christmas Past

Welcome Christmas, bring your cheer.
Cheer to all Whos far and near.
Christmas day is in our grasp,

> So long as we have hands to clasp.
> Christmas day will always be,
> Just as long as we have we.
> > How the Grinch Stole Christmas (TV Version)
> > Dr. Seuss

It was last year, the day after the big snow. Big snow in these parts means two inches, but Yankees be damned, we were going to enjoy this one because it was a week before Christmas and the weather geeks were forecasting more snow. We hadn't had a white Christmas in this part of North Carolina since time out of mind, and as I crossed the library parking lot, which was a solid sheet of white and quiet as a church on Monday, I could feel the sentiment that the Christmas snow brought with it. It was a sweet feeling, innocent. It gave everything sort of a simple, old fashioned, childlike feel to it. For me it brought back the taste of hot chocolate, the smell of oranges and real pine needles and that excitement you could feel in the pit of your stomach knowing that Christmas was only a week away. For me that feeling had long been dormant, driven to the farthest, darkest corner of my mind by noise, flashing lights and false electronic happiness. It had gone there when the Christmas shopping season had started in July and the birth of Christ had taken a back seat to selling toys.

The bad thing about good feelings like that is that they don't last long. That day the feeling ended as soon as Bill unlocked the front doors and the same patrons, who are waiting every morning, walked in out of the snow and stomped up the stairs. Over the next hour the same man locked up the same computer three times chatting with Mrs. Claus in her boudoir. Then some home school mom clogged up the copier with red construction paper and a teenager wanted a book on Nostradamus because she had heard that he had made a prediction that Fidel Castro would defect to America to become a department store Santa Claus. I had just gotten her a book off the shelf when the fight started.

Dr. Marion Walsh is a retired urologist. He's about two years older than baseball and usually he's in the library every day to monopolize the *Wall Street Journal*. For awhile there though, he had taken a shine to the JC Penney Wish Book that one of the staff had brought in and put on the rack. Rufus is a street preacher/cursing derelict who accompanies Purdie Mae Pierce to the library with the same regularity. While Purdie Mae is cussing out the staff and photo copying her fake jewelry, Rufus reads every page of every magazine on the rack.

They both are in the library on a daily basis, but they have never had any contact with each other until that day when Rufus took the doctor's beloved catalog right from under his nose while he took his 10:30 nap. In trying to get it back, Walsh snatched the book, along with Rufus's hat, the one that says "Women Want Me, Fish Fear Me" and the fight was on. Rufus is hard of hearing and talks with the volume of a jet taking off. The doctor has a speech impediment and almost constant, often resonant flatulence, so round one, in sheer entertainment value, made the Thrilla in Manila seem like an afternoon of watching paint dry. It was loud, if not funny, especially to a gaggle of teenage girls pretending to study at a table nearby.

The head of reference, Frank Miner, broke up the fight. It took a good fifteen minutes and he got slapped in the face with Rufus's hat on top of that. The ruckus ended with Dr. Walsh stomping out and Frank was ticked by the time he got back to the reference desk. He said something about jerking a knot in somebody's pucker string and stormed on by toward his office.

I was watching Frank (you could hear him swearing all the way back to his cubicle) and didn't notice Ronnie Moffitt walk around the reference desk and come up behind me. Ronnie, to put it quite bluntly, is a pain in the butt. He's one of those patrons most of the staff would murder each other over to keep from waiting on, and when Julie Bray saw him pass the circulation desk and head my way, she heard nature call and vanished as well.

I turned to face Ronnie, stone-faced as usual and again decked out in camouflage and black, which was his custom. Ronnie's always very secretive about what he talks with the librarians about, so he comes around the desk rather than leaning over it like everybody else, and stands real close so you're always sure to get a nose full of Redman and Old Spice. I took a step back and put on my best glad-to-see-you face.

"Hey, Ronnie, can I help you?" He took a step forward and we were together again. What made it worse was that I was backed up against a stool and I couldn't get away again without making it obvious.

"You look on the Internet for that fella's name that I give you? Do a background check like you said you could on there?" I thought for awhile, trying to decide what he was talking about, which wasn't always easy, and then it finally clicked.

"No, I looked all afternoon one day last week and I couldn't find anything. Most of those sites that do background checks charge a..."

"I didn't think you was. You want to know who that is?"

"Uh."

"He's a Fed. You know, government. He's been following me about a year now."

"Okay I..."

"I don't know who he is or who he's with. Justice Department, CIA, NSA I don't know and it don't matter. All I know is that he's after me." It was then that I dug myself in even deeper and I've kicked myself ever since.

"What did you do?"

"I didn't do nothing. I don't know why they're following me, but they've bugged my house, my car, they intercept my e-mails, steal my paper. They've even put these little cameras in all the light fixtures in the house. They got 'em behind the bathroom mirror too."

"Why..."

"You know who he looks like?" I didn't, but Ronnie told me anyway. "He's a big fellow with a bushy beard. Look's a lot like that fella that writes them SEAL team books. What his name? Maraschino?"

"Marcinko."

"That's him, and who knows? He was really a SEAL wasn't he?"

"That's..."

"Again, it don't matter. I'm on to him. I didn't think that you would find anything on him or whoever's after me, but I thought that I'd try. I'm sorry that I asked you. You know they might come after you too, now that they've seen you talking to me."

"I'll be careful."

"You see that van parked across the road?" I looked through the reading room, and I could see through the window that there was a gray van parked across the street in front of Bender Real Estate. It looked like it had been primered and it had a white pattern on it that made it looked tie-dyed.

"Yeah."

"That's them. They're listening to everything we say with this high tech surveillance equipment and they're tied in to these reconnaissance satellites that can zoom in and watch people. They've got infrared, ultraviolet, they can see right through the roof of this place. I know they're watching us now." I did a really stupid thing then, but it was a reflex and I paid for it. I looked up. "Don't do that, fool! You want them to know who you are? What you look like? I've got to get out of here. I parked about two miles away at the Harris Teeter. I'm gonna wait and leave the building with a big crowd of people and then I'll sneak through people's backyards till I get back to the truck, and take the long way home. If they do catch me, I'm gonna make 'em work for it." Ronnie started out then, walking like a man on a mission. Just before he left through the double doors and headed for the stairs, we made eye contact and he gave me this real slow solemn nod like we shared a secret.

"Give 'em hell, Ronnie," I said. I'm so glad he didn't hear me.

Early that afternoon while I was in the lounge taking the batteries out of a singing Christmas tree that somebody had set up back there, Julie waited on these two guys who showed up at the desk. They had cement all over their blue jeans and dirty t-shirts over long underwear tops. They were wearing Santa hats and one was holding a Styrofoam coffee cup with a lid on it.

"Where are your bug books?" one started to ask, but his buddy finished the question before he could.

"What specifically are you looking for?"

"Well, we found this bug on the job site this morning. It was in the house we're working on, and seeing as it's as cold as it is and it's still alive, we thought that it was a little weird and none of us had seen one like it before. We thought that maybe y'all'd have a book or something that would have it in it." Before she could say anything more the other man held up the cup. "You wanna see it?" Now Julie doesn't like bugs so I'm sure she didn't, but she's a trooper and agreed so that they could identify the bug more easily. She said that it was a strange looking bug. It was about three inches long including the antennae that waved slowly back and forth, giving the only evidence that the thing was still alive. It was a color of brown that would have blended in against wood or in trees.

"I think that we've got something that can help you right out here," she said, going into reference for Grzimek's Animal Life Encyclopedia, the insect volume two, I believe it is. They all three gathered around and she began to flip through the pages. Some of them have full color plates showing various kinds of insects, but nothing jumped out at them right off. They looked for several minutes and Julie actually thumbed through the volume twice and was just about to try something else when she looked beside her and saw that one of the men had taken the bug out and let it sit in his hand.

"Thought we could give you a better look," he said, and held it down just inches between her face and the pages of the book. She straightened up and kind of slid away.

"I think that we've got another book that we can check out in the circulating collection if you'll let me..."

"Hey, there it is!" said the other man who put a dirty finger down between the pages and pointed to a picture that did look like the insect that was now crawling up the other man's arm.

"Oh," she said and read the information out to them. "It says here that it's an Assassin Bug, *Rhynocoris iracundis*." She read on about habitat, size, behavior, mating habits, blah, blah, blah ... until she turned the page and considered shutting the book right there.

"It say anything else?" asked the bug man.

"Well, it says that the assassin bug produces a protozoa that can enter the body through the bite, other wounds, or through the mucus membranes in the eyes and produce a syndrome known as Chagas disease in which the heart, thyroid gland and nervous system can be damaged, although usually in children, and can be fatal."

"Whoa," said the other man.

"Damn!" shouted the bug man and flipped the bug off his hand where it soared over Julie's shoulder and landed on the floor. "Oh, Man, sorry. We'll get it." Both men pushed by her and began chasing the bug which darted into the corner next to where the bound magazines are kept.

I had gotten back from break while they were looking through the book and was helping a patron find a copy of *Skipping Christmas*. I could hear shouting along with the sound of feet stomping and bound volumes of magazines being slapped against the floor. As we made our way down the aisle I heard a particularly vicious flurry, followed a few seconds later by one final hard slap and a voice that said, "Got 'em! You got a Kleenex?" My patron wrinkled up her nose as I handed her the book.

"Do we really want to know?"

She thought for a second and then shook her head. She smiled and thanked me as I followed her down the aisle. I was walking through the stacks when I looked at the shelf on my left and saw someone looking between the books at me. I guess it was because I had helped someone find one of the Marcinko books before break, but for a second I thought of what Ronnie had told me that morning. Whoever it was, he was tall, had a beard and eyes like those I had seen from the spine of one of the SEAL Force books or whatever he calls them. For one brief second I thought that Ronnie was right, that this man had not only come after Ronnie, but me as well. Neither of us had done anything, but he was here and for one moment I just knew that he had drawn a gun, one with a silencer. At any minute I would hear that weird sound like those type of guns make in spy movies, and as I walked down the aisle, a bullet would come through the shelves. It would hurl past Kinky Friedman, Grisham and Hemingway and strike me down in the E through Ks. I hurried to the end of the aisle, maybe to see who it was, maybe to get away and as I hurried past the end of the next aisle I heard somebody call, "'Scuse me. Could I get some help here?"

I looked in that direction and saw this very short man standing on a stool to get to one of the higher shelves. He had a beard but it was a great deal shorter and neater looking than I had imagined, and the eyes I had seen glaring down at me looked out from behind a pair of bottle bottomed glasses. As he got down and walked over to me, a bell that he wore around his neck jingled. He looked even more timid and grandfatherly and I had to smile as he asked me for a biography of Sam Ervin. I got him his book, flashed him my best friendly neighborhood librarian smile and even shook his hand. I could have kissed him.

As we closed up and left that evening I was ready to go home, but I was sort of sad that I didn't get that old Christmas feeling back as we headed back through the snow to where our cars were parked. I was walking with my head down, and when I looked up to step over the curb, I spotted Ronnie Moffitt sitting in his pickup truck, which was parked over by the staff vehicles. He was in disguise, or I guess that was what he was trying to do. He was wearing a really bad, obviously cheap Santa Claus suit. The hat was way too small and it sat on his head like a dunce cap. The beard was small as well and real ratty looking, like Ronnie had just stuck some cotton balls to his face and that was it. The mustache was crooked, and while the left side drooped down to cover the corner of his mouth, the other pointed up his nose. To top off the ensemble he was wearing some Richard Petty wrap around sunglasses. Our gazes met and he gave me another slow, knowing Clint Eastwood nod which I returned, all the while biting my lip trying hard not to laugh.

While I was getting into my car, Ronnie pulled out and passed me so that I followed him out of the parking lot. He turned right up Main Street and while I was pulling out and starting left, I saw the van in my rear view mirror, the gray one with the tie-dyed paint job, pull out of the apartment complex next door and follow him up the street.

Late Christmas Eve I sat up with my daughter who was too excited to sleep. All the lights in the house were off and the only illumination we had were the lights on the tree and the television, as *How the Grinch Stole Christmas!* played itself out for the twelfth time in less than a week. As she finally dozed off and the credits started to roll I looked out the window. The snow was all gone. The temperatures that day had been in the sixties, so no more came to take its place. My neighbor's house was decked out in multicolored flickering lights from eve to foundation and I could still hear the boom boom boom of someone's car stereo as it faded into the distance. It was there on the couch with my daughter's head on my chest surrounded by all the tacky trappings of a twenty-first century Christmas that the feeling came back. The taste of hot chocolate, the smell of pine and oranges and that excitement that you can feel in the pit of your stomach knowing that Christmas is here.

Appendix B: A Letter to Library Patrons or Prospective Patrons

Dear Sir or Madam,

    The next time you are in our libraries, if we are too busy, distracted, or for any reason fail to welcome you, please know that it means the world to us that you are there. We might fail to let you know this. There are times we might not realize it ourselves, but we want you to come through our doors. We want you to check out material. We want you to use our computers.

    There is one thing that I personally would like to ask, and I think there are a great deal of other librarians who would like to see this as well. That is, I would like for all of you to keep an open mind with regard to the materials and services you will find here. When you look at all the books on our shelves, when you look at all the movies that we have here, all the magazines and then all the information that the Internet gives us the access to, we can quite literally give you the world. We wish that you would think of that before you spend your time here on Facebook or playing video games, before heading out of our doors back to your life elsewhere. There has to be a subject you are interested in that doesn't involve poking someone or lining up pieces of fruit on an online video game. Whatever interests you, whatever information that might be tickling the back of your brain, if you will give us a little patience and a little effort, we will find you that information, and what then? Do you glance over that book, look at that magazine article and then toss it into the corner before you go back to *Call of Duty?* I hope not, I hope that this little tidbit will lead to another one and another one and another. Maybe this will lead to a love of finding these little facts and what a love for finding out little facts is called is education.

Appendix B: A Letter to Library Patrons or Prospective Patrons

When I was still working at the college library I had a gentleman, a member of the general public, come in and want every bit of information on a lamassu. A lamassu is an Assyrian deity often depicted with a bull or lion's body, an eagle's wings and a human's head. This was a subject that interested him and he carried with him an entire binder full of information on this particular mythological creature. Did this do him any good? No, I'm sure that it didn't put any money in his pocket. It didn't make him a success in whatever profession he chose to pursue. No, it exercised his mind and it might have started an interest in questions and the search to find the answers to those questions. Someone asked me once if reading *King Lear* did anybody any good. That if reading *A Midsummer Night's Dream* is any more important than, say, covering a chair. This person saw the chair as a more important endeavor because he could potentially make more of a living at it. Does reading *King Lear* or researching a lamassu do you any good? Yes, it does. It encourages something called thinking which encourages something called expanding your mind, and expanded minds will change the world.

Everybody wants change. That's all I hear, see, or read in the paper. Nobody likes the way things are and everybody wants change. Well I hate to tell you this, but change won't come from those guys and girls who promise it every time they run for office. They're too comfortable with the way things are, so you should know that they won't. They'll say they do, and they might make some sort of visible allowance, but it won't change anything. It won't improve your life. No, real change is going to come from you. I should say that real change will come from you provided you read, you learn and you expand your mind beyond what's happening on Facebook. Just doing the same thing every day, going through the motions of living, taking things by what you hear from the talking heads, from the media and from the people in charge waiting for that check from them just so you can do the same thing the following day, the following week and the following month, won't change anything. We want to help you read. We want to help you educate yourself. We want to help you get training and find gainful employment. That's what we want to see. A few months ago when the library where I work had two patrons find jobs that they had found and achieved using our computers, we couldn't have been happier. We like to see people on our computers applying for employment, taking online classes or sitting in the corner studying, but most of all we want you here. Come in and get on Facebook, or play *Minecraft* if you want to, but after you're done, stick around and poke through the books, read the newspapers, check something out and take it with you. Just be sure and bring it back. Oh yeah. Please don't yell at us or poop on our floor.

Sincerely,
The Librarians

Appendix C: A Letter to My Fellow Librarians

I have a scenario for you. It didn't really happen, I just made it up. I love to people watch, and sometimes I'll attach a scenario to one person or a couple. I do it when I'm out somewhere and I'm bored, waiting on my wife for some reason. In this particular scenario there is a small branch library sitting on the outskirts of a city park. There is a new librarian and in the first few days of being at his new position he decides that he wants to do a little marketing for the library, so he walks out into the park with a handful of brochures from his place of employment. He approaches a group of kids just walking off one of the basketball courts, hands them a brochure and tells them that he would like to talk to them about a few of the programs available at the local library.

"No thanks, man," the kid says in a very condescending tone. I don't read much, and if I do I'll just order something from Amazon." The librarian is non-deterred, and tries to tell the young man about the movies available on DVD at the library.

"It's called YouTube dude, or I'll get it from Netflix." He then tries to tell the young man about the reference services, but he is told that he already knows how to use Google. Every time he tried to sell the virtues of the library to this young man, his efforts were shot down, with the responses getting more condescending all the time. Finally he goes back to the library discouraged, and maybe a little irritated. Within the hour the librarian is on the desk and the same young man comes in, basketball under his arm and his friends in tow.

"Hey man, where's the bathroom?"

"Have you checked the Internet?"

The reason I am relating this little yarn to you is to illustrate a view that some people have concerning libraries. If it's available at the library, it's available on the Internet. These are the same people that are convinced that whatever they see on the Internet is true. If you are new to the profession, be prepared to hear this. Just remember that these people don't know what they are talking about and that the profession you have just entered into is one that this still relevant.

If you are in any way like me, there are times when you will get discouraged. You will spend your day at the reference desk and check people into the computer just so they can flirt with the opposite sex on Facebook or play games. During these times those words will keep coming back to you. "I can just check Google." "Libraries are just over-glorified Internet cafes." I've heard that one to. Just keep reminding yourself that at least those people are there, and from what statistics are telling us, there are a lot of people coming into libraries, whatever the reason. Statistics show that Americans go to libraries—school, public and academic— nearly three times more often than they go to the movies. In 2011 there was a total of 16,604 libraries, including branches, which means that there are more libraries than McDonald's, and academic libraries alone will answer 56.1 million reference questions a year. This is almost 10 million more people than attend college football games.

People always have misconceptions about the services that libraries provide. Of course what immediately comes to mind are books. After that, the library is a place where you get questions answered, then Internet access and maybe next is movies. What libraries are really providing the public, not to sound dramatic, is freedom. Over the last few months two guys who have been coming in our library religiously have used our computers to find jobs. That gives them a certain amount of financial freedom. We also have patrons come in and use our libraries to study for classes they are taking to further their education, or get on computers to take the classes themselves. School and academic libraries have an even more active role in educating people. This all gives them more opportunity to not only find better and higher paying employment in the future, but also gives them the tools to think for themselves.

When a patron comes into the library, whether it's to do some intensive research, check out a novel or harvest their crops on some Facebook video game, they are there in the building, the same building where we have all those methods for a person educating himself. That education, and the expansion of the mind that follows, is where that patron will find true freedom. The ability to look at things, to read and to study for themselves rather than take some talking head on television's word for it is what a library provides. Everybody wants change and that is the best way to go about it—for everybody to fill their minds with something other than celebrity gossip and sawdust. This is true freedom and it's available for free at any library. All you have to do is come in the door and take the initiative to poke around in what we have here. The second end is a great deal harder than the first, but you, dear librarian, can be the vessel for that.

What I'm trying to say in my own rambling way, is that you are important. Despite what people may tell you throughout your career, you are important. Important to this country, important to this world and, on a personal level, important to me. When I started this book I started thinking that when my wife and I found out that we were going to have children, each time a librarian was one of the first few people who heard the news. In fact my oldest daughter was only a few days old when a gaggle of librarians burst into our room, passed her around like a bottle of cheap whiskey and then left. When I found out that my nephew had died in a car crash at age 20, one of the biggest tragedies of my life, a librarian was there when I got the news. A few years later I watched the World Trade Center fall with librarians. So you can see how this profession, and the people in it, have shaped my life, for the better, and it is my ardent belief that you will shape our world for the better. Now go forth, my comrades, and spread knowledge. Make it available and give it to your patrons. Maybe they won't want to take it, but just keep it dangling there like bait for a fish. They'll have to come up for air some time.

Bibliography

Battles, Matthew. *Library: An Unquiet History.* New York: W.W. Norton, 2004. Print.
Brenner, Nancy F. *Randolph Public Library and Its Community: A Community—Library Analysis.* Asheboro, N.C., 1979. Print.
Carmichael, James V., Jr. "Innovation in Library Education: Historical X-Files on Technology, People, and Change." *North Carolina Libraries* 56 (1998): 28–35. Print.
Eberhart, George M. *The Whole Library Handbook: Current Data, Professional Advice, and Curiosa about Libraries and Library Services.* Chicago: American Library Association, 1991. Print.
Lerner, Frederick Andrew, Stuart B. Schimmel, and Caroline F. Schimmel. *The Story of Libraries: From the Invention of Writing to the Computer Age.* New York: Continuum, 2001. Print.
Martin, Cheryl Lynn. *The Heritage of Randolph County, North Carolina.* Asheboro, N.C.: Randolph County Heritage Book Committee, in Cooperation with the Heritage Book Collection and Delmar Printing, 1993. Print.
Memory, Marjorie Whittington. "A History of the Randolph Public Library, 1935–1967." Master's thesis, University of North Carolina at Chapel Hill, 1968. Print.
Roy, Janice. "The Search Starts Here." *Courier Tribune* [Asheboro] 18 February 1996: n.p. Print.
Rubin, Richard. *Foundations of Library and Information Science.* New York: Neal-Schuman, 2004. Print.
Schulman, Neil. "Knovel Blog: 5 Fun Facts You May Not Know About Libraries." *Knovel Blog RSS.* 13 June 2011. Web. 22 May 2014.

Index

Advanced Research Projects Agency (ARPA) 83
Akkadian (language) 32
Alexander the Great 33, 35
Alexandria, Egypt 33
Al-Hakam II 42
Alley Oop 103
Al-Ma'mun (Caliphate) 41
Al-Mutanabi (poet) 40
Amir ibn al As (general) 33
The Andy Griffith Show 55, 159
Anheuser-Busch Company 22
An Lu-shan (general) 39
"Anne" 26, 27
Apollodorus 36
Aramaic (language) 32
Aretino, Pietro 86
ARPAnet 83
Assyrian (language) 32
Athenaeum 46
Augustus (emperor) 35
Aurelian (Roman emperor) 34
Austen, Jane 152

"Backfield in Motion" (song) 21
Baghdad 41, 42, 43
Balalaika 165
Balzac, Honore de 48
Batman ('60s TV series) 16
Berners-Lee, Tim 83
Bibliothèque Nationale 37
The Big Sleep (film) 13, 15
Blue, Thomas Fountion 49
Bogart, Humphrey 13, 15
Bohemia 16, 22
The Bold and the Beautiful 166

Bones (college friend) 146, 148
Boston Public Library 47, 50
Boy's Town 14
Branch Davidians 19
The Brief Reign of Pharaoh Ho-Ho and the Queen of Denial (play) 136–143
Buck (derelict) 108, 109
Budweiser 22
Buffy the Vampire Slayer 18, 51

Caesar, Julius 34, 35
The Caliph Omar 33
Call of Duty (video game) 175
Carnegie, Andrew 49
Carter, Jimmy 21
Casanova, Giacomo Girolamo 16, 22
Caulfield, Holden 122
Cerf, Vinton 83
Ceske Budejovice (city) 16, 22
Chang'an (city) 39
Cheney, Dick 89
Ch'eng Chu 40
Ch'eng Ti (emperor) 38
Ch'ien Dynasty 40
Ch'ien-lung (emperor) 40
Chin Dynasty 37
Chou Dynasty 37
A Christmas Carol 112
chuanqui 39
Circulating Libraries 46
Citizen Kane 13
"Clark" 25
Clinton, Bill 19
Clower, Jerry 23

Codex (bound book) 36, 41, 85
Confucius 37–39
Constantine (emperor) 35, 36
Constantinople 42
Cordova 42
Cos (city) 36
Le Coucher de la Mariée (film) 87
Crapper, Thomas 151
Curtin, Jane 17
Czech Republic 16, 22

Daguerre, Louis 86
daguerreotype 86
Damascus 42
Dangerfield, Rodney 97
Dar al-Ilm (libraries) 41, 42
"Dean" Clower 23
de Cisneros, Cardinal Francisco Ximinez 43
Desk Set 18
Dewey, Melville 47
Diocles 36
"Dirt Bike Old Man" 114
"Dr. Beauregard" 60
Doubt (film) 14
Duck Dynasty 25
Duke University 27
Dumbledore, Albus 114

L'Ecole des filles (novel) 86
Extension Department 57, 116

Facebook 175–178
Fahrenheit 451 37
Family Guy 11
Farlow, George 96

Index

Farlow, Michael 93
Farlow, Nathan 96
Farlow, Ruth 96
Farlow, Thomas 96
Farlow family 96
Fayetteville State University 146
Fielding, Henry 48
Fife, Barney 78
Fifty Shades of Grey 48
Five Classics 37, 38
Flaubert, Gustave 48
"The Flying Cowboy" 114
Foundations of Library and Information Science 45, 49
Four Little Girls 109
Franklin, Benjamin 16, 46
Franklin, John Hope 49
Frasier, Brendan 17
Funk and Wagnalls 119, 164

Game of Thrones 40
Gent, Peter 44
The Ghost of Christmas Past (short story) 167–173
Ghostbusters 27
Globe Theater 104
The Godfather (book) 21
Good News 13
Google 177, 178
Gordian Knot 33
Gordon, Barbara (Batgirl, Oracle) 50
Graduate Record Exam 60
Grand Mosque of Damascus 42
Guns and Roses 19

Hadley, Marian 49
Haithcock, Marsha 108
Han Dynasty 38
Harvard, John 45, 50
Harvard University 50
Hepburn, Katharine 18
High Point University 22
Hoffman, Philip Seymour 14
Hogwarts School of Witchcraft and Wizardry 114
Holmes, Sherlock 152
Hoover, J. Edgar 16
Hopkins, Anthony 33
Hunger Games 147
Hustler 87
Hypatia (philosopher) 34
Imperial Library of China 39, 40

Indiana Jones and the Last Crusade 15
Iowa Caucus 21

Italian Renaissance 86
It's a Wonderful Life 13

Jack Daniels 22
Jack the Ripper 152
Jamaica Inn (film) 14
James, Dell 19
The Jungle Book (film) 94
Jurassic Park (book) 27
Jurched Hordes 40

Kaa (cartoon character) 94, 95
Kane, Carol 152
Kercheval, Margaret 49
"The Killer Tomato" 114
The King and Queen 59
King Lear (play) 176
The Koran 40, 41, 42

Lamassu 176
The Last Exorcism 14
Left Behind 36
Leo V the Armenian (emperor) 41
Lerner, Fred 37
The Librarian 17, 18, 51
The Library at Alexandria 33, 34
Library Services and Construction Act 50
Lindsey, Hal 53
Lin-t'ai ku-hih (book: *A Tale of the National Library*) 40
"The Little Fuhrer" 23
Liu Hsiang 38
Liu Hsin 38
"Lone Strummer" 115
"Looking Down at the Grass Man" 114
Louisville Free Public Library 49
Lumière Brothers 87
Luoyang (city) 39

Manchuria 40
Manson, Marilyn 163
Mao Tse-Tung 16
Mayberry 56, 145, 158
McAllister, Slobber 115, 116, 122–135
McConaughey, Matthew 21
Mercantile Library 46
"The Micro Manager" 29, 30
A Midsummer Night's Dream (play) 176
Miller, Donna 108
Minecraft (video game) 176
"Miss Terri" 84
"Mr. Benz" 77, 81, 94, 95, 112, 147, 170

"Mr. Duncan" 55–57, 76, 81, 85, 94, 165
Mister Rogers' Neighborhood 14
Mitchem, Robert 14
I Modi 86
Mohenjo-Dao, Pakistan 151
Mongols 43
Monsters University 11, 14
Mosul 41
Mountain Man 114
MUFON 146
Muhammad I 42
The Mummy (1999 film) 16, 51
The Music Man 14

Negro Branch Library (Nashville, Tennessee) 49
Newhart, Bob 17, 165
The Night of the Hunter 14
Nixon, Doug 162
North Dallas Forty 44
November Rain: short story 19; song 19

Octavia 35
Oh Christmas Tree (short story) 118–121

P. Diddy (Puff Daddy) 21
Papillion (book) 21
Parallel Lives (book) 34
Penthouse 87
Peterborough, New Hampshire 46, 50
Phantom Poers 152
The Philadelphia Story 13, 14
Playboy 87
Plutarch 34
Pope Clement VIII 86
Porky's 2 14, 51
pornography 86
Poundstone, Paula 11, 12
Pratchett, Terry 50
Ptolemaic Dynasty 33
Ptolemy I 33
Ptolemy XIII 34
"Purple Brown Suit Wolverine" 114
Pyle, Gomer 160

Queenie 64–66, 106–112, 115, 144, 163

"The Rabbi" (college friend) 30, 31, 146, 147
Ragionamenti (novel) 86
Raimondi, Marcantonio (printer) 86
Rats (short story) 122–135

Index

Reconquista (historical period) 43
Romano, Giulio (artist) 86
Rothman, John 12
Royal Library of Alexandria 33
Rubin, Richard E. 45, 47, 49
Rufus (police chief) 31
Rule of St. Benedict 36
"The Running Man" 28, 29

Sabur ibn Ardashir 41
Saladin 43
The Satanic Bible 21
Scott (college friend) 30, 147
The Searchers (film) 44
Seduction of the Innocent (book) 16
Seinfeld 14, 160
Seles, Monica 19
Sesame Street 21
The Sex Pistols (band) 27
Sherman, Gen. William Tecumseh 101
16th Street Baptist Church 109
Slaughterhouse-Five (book) 21
Slobber McAllister 115, 122–135

Smothers Brothers 96
"social library" 46
I Sonetti Lussuriosi (novel) 86
Sophie's Choice 12
Sputnik I 83
Ssu-k'u ch'u nan-shu (book: *Complete Library of the Four Treasures*) 40
Starsky and Hutch 114
State Library Commission 58
Stewart, Jimmy 13
Stone, Oliver 33
The Story of Libraries (book) 37
Streep, Meryl 12
Sui Dynasty 38, 39
Sumerians 32, 34, 78

Tang Dynasty 39
Theophilus (bishop) 34
Tiberius 35
Tijuana Bibles 87
Tracy, Spencer 14, 18
Trajan (emperor) 35
Transmission Control Protocol 83
Twin Peaks 158
"Two Tons of Fun" 84

Ugaritic (language) 32
Umayyad Caliphate 43
Unseen University 50

Vespasian (emperor) 35
Von Waldstein, Count Joseph Karl 16

Wake Forest Demon Deacons 57
Waqf (endowment) 41
Wayne, John 44
Weisz, Rachel 16
Wertham, Fredric 16
Works Progress Administration (WPA) 58
Wu Ti (emperor) 38
Wyle, Noah 17

"Yellow Wolverine" 114
The Young and the Restless 166

Zappa, Frank 114
Zodiac Killer 152
Zola, Emile 48

www.ingramcontent.com/pod-product-compliance
Ingram Content Group UK Ltd.
Pitfield, Milton Keynes, MK11 3LW, UK
UKHW050523150426
5217IPUK00026B/1769